THE BEST OF ELVIS

By Cindy Hazen & Mike Freeman

Fifteen percent of all profits to benefit
St. Jude Children's Research Hospital

*Marilyn
Thank you!
Mike Freeman
1-26-03*

Also by Cindy Hazen and Mike Freeman

The Whole Elvis Tour—
A Visitor's Guide To the King's Memphis

THE BEST OF ELVIS

RECOLLECTIONS OF
A GREAT HUMANITARIAN

Cindy Hazen
Mike Freeman

Memphis Explorations
Memphis, Tennessee

Library of Congress Catalog Card Number 92-060186

ISBN: 0-9632274-0-8

Cover design by Cindy Hazen & Mike Freeman
Front cover image courtesy of AP Wide World Photos
Back cover image courtesy of Linda Everett
Text design by Cindy Hazen & Mike Freeman
Typesetting by CST Typo-Graphics: Memphis, TN

Manufactured in the United States of America

First Edition: May 1992

10 9 8 7 6 5 4 3

IN MEMORY OF
Robert Hazen

It's time to remind those who are not his greatest fans that the biggest part of Elvis Presley is his heart; it is full of love for everyone.

—Danny Thomas.

Contents

Acknowledgements

Everyone has to start somewhere. This is our first book. At times it has seemed an enormous undertaking. We've spent countless evenings and weekends working on this project as we've juggled full-time jobs and family obligations. There were times when our self-imposed deadline seemed impossible to meet. But Elvis is a subject that is absorbing, eternally fascinating. The long hours barely seemed like work. As we pored over newspaper clippings and delved deeper into Elvis' life, we lost ourselves in the legend. At times it was difficult to put aside to attend to our other responsibilities.

We would not have been successful in reaching our goals if it had not been for the help of many people, all of whom took the risk of dealing with two unknown authors. First of all, we want to thank Don and Karen Wilson for opening a lot of doors for us. Don is President of the "Elvis Presley Network" which is committed to preserving Elvis' memory. His and Karen's knowledge of Elvis and collection of memorabilia is tremendous. We thank them for trusting us, sharing little-known stories, introducing us to their friends, and for giving us use of their unpublished photographs. Their friendship means a lot to us.

Richard Davis met us in the "Elvis room" at Alfred's one night during George Klein's show. It was a meeting we think of often. It's been said that of all of Elvis' friends, he is the most like him. The stories he told were moving; of a side of Elvis few people are aware of. We left that night thinking of the incredible man Elvis was. And in Elvis' style, Richard made us feel special.

Janelle McComb is an inspiration and her stories held us spellbound. She shared with us the Elvis she knew: the man, not the celebrity. With her, we feel that Elvis had true friends.

We want to thank Eddie Fadal for trusting us and sharing some of his experiences with Elvis. Eddie described events of 1958 so vividly we almost felt as though we were there.

We also want to thank Joe Kent and Will McDaniel (Bardahl) who shared their memories of Elvis. We wish Joe the best of luck in his acting career and Bardahl success with his new fan club, the "Elvis Worldwide Fan Club" of Memphis.

The following people assisted us with our research on the "Ten Outstanding Young Men of America" award: Tim Miller, President of the Memphis Jaycees; Frank Taylor, chairman of the event; Harold Sterling, co-chairman; and Barbara McAlpin, who met Elvis at the convention.

We are thankful for the people who shared stories with us: George Klein (who teaches us during his shows at Marlowe's), D.J. Fontana, Mary Jenkins, John Tate (Gary Pepper's cousin), Roger Fakes, Ursula and Bob Egger, and Arlene Cogan Bradley.

We are extremely grateful to Graceland for the use of photographs from the Colonel Parker collection. Special thanks go to Steve Marshall for bearing with us as we tried to choose from their tremendous selection. We also want to thank Todd Morgan and Patsy Andersen who both took time out of very busy schedules to assist us. Patsy has been a tremendous help and her words of encouragement have meant a lot to us.

The following people have our deep appreciation for use of their photographs: Linda Everett (who operates a great photo club for fans); Terry Wood (for his fabulous shots of the Tupelo appearance); Jim Montgomery (of *The Shreveport Times*); Langston McEachern (for Hayride photographs); *The Honolulu Star Bulletin* (for the rare pictures of events preceding the famous '61 concert); *The Honolulu Advertiser* (for photos of the USS Arizona concert); and Memphis State University (for use of photos from the Mississippi Valley Collection.)

We also wish to thank the following individuals for providing insight into their organizations: Marler Stone of the Elvis Presley Memorial Trauma Center; Paul Hollahan of Le Bonheur Children's Hospital; and Paul Parham of St. Jude Children's Research Hospital who also shared the photo of Elvis and Danny Thomas aboard the "Potomac".

The librarians in Memphis and Tupelo deserve our thanks for allowing us to delve through clippings files and tie up the copy machines for hours on end. Other librarians across the country have been kind enough to do that work for us.

Many Elvis fans have supported us with our efforts, and we want to thank a few in particular: Alice Schlichte for her inspirational letters. We pray you may continue to enjoy full days and continue the work for the children. Bill De Night for his help in promoting our booklet and for the tremendous work he does for Le Bonheur and the Trauma Center. Robin Rosaaen for meeting with us and providing us with some great information. We doubt there's a greater PR person around, and look forward to spending more time together during her next visit to Memphis. Priscilla Parker for her great newsletters; Betty Hicks for her help and warm welcome into The Then, Now and Forever Fan Club; Mary Cartaya for her kindness and support. We love you, Mary. And, last but certainly not least, Becky Smith for her encouragement, and most of all, her friendship. We're so glad she wrote to us.

Finally, we wish to thank Bill Burk for his advice on self-publishing and marketing. Bill has a flair for storytelling and we thoroughly enjoyed listening to his experiences. We appreciate the use of his personal photographs and wish him the best of luck with his projects.

Foreword

*N*o other entertainer has captured the world's attention as Elvis Presley has. His first name is recognized in every language and his fans are found in the farthest corners of the globe. Almost every day Elvis is mentioned in print or on television. If not the subject of a feature, references to Elvis are made in sitcoms or unrelated news articles. He's become a symbol of American culture.

Life magazine, in 1990, selected Elvis Presley as one of the hundred most influential Americans during the twentieth century. But *Life* was not the only member of the media to recognize his impact. In 1969 the *Sunday Times* of London listed Elvis as one of a thousand people throughout the world who changed our culture. At that time he was only thirty-four years old.

What was most remarkable about Elvis Presley was how he managed to make such an impact at such a young age. He recorded for Sun Records at the ages of nineteen and twenty. Music critics and historians consider those songs the birth of the now multi-billion dollar rock music industry. Elvis Presley's breakthrough gold records and films began in 1956, when Elvis was just twenty-one.

There is no simple explanation for the influence Elvis Presley exerted, except that he had enormous talent and a powerful presence. His charisma defied the limitations of print, screen, and recordings. His impact is felt as strongly today as it was during his career. Jerry Hopkins, an Elvis biographer, wrote in 1972 that America had four unique cultural contributions to the world: Coca-Cola, baseball, Mickey Mouse and Elvis Presley. It's a difficult honor to bear. Elvis was not just a cultural icon, but a human being with ordinary human qualities.

He was called the "King of Rock and Roll," a title which disturbed him. When a fan presented him with a gold crown and said, "This is for you; you're the King," he gently corrected her. "No honey," he said. "Christ is the King. I'm just a singer." Elvis never lost his faith in God. And he was troubled that some might have believed he was anything more than human. He never intended for anyone to adore him.

Elvis once said, "It's very hard to live up to an image." He lived in a world that watched his every move. His critics expected perfection in every act. Every performance was supposed to be brilliant. Each decision to record or act had to be profoundly right. In his later years, he was continually compared to his youth and his earlier successes. It's doubtful anyone could satisfy all of the demands placed upon Elvis Presley. If he failed at all, it was that he could not live up to his image. He made very human choices. He aged. Perhaps it was frightening, as much for his critics as for himself: if Elvis reached middle age, then we all must be losing part of our youth.

Elvis has become the target of cruel jokes and tasteless books. Even in his hometown, the strength of his family, friends, and admirers is tested. In October 1991, the Greater Mid-South Junior Chamber of Commerce (not to be confused with the Memphis Jaycees — a separate chapter) depicted Elvis in a coffin surrounded by empty pizza boxes and jelly donuts. One wonders why people who are normally considerate of others show no compassion when it comes to Elvis. Perhaps, because he's a cultural icon, he's lost his identity as a man. He's viewed as a commodity, as though he has always been inanimate. That he was flesh and blood, and still has family members living in Memphis, is forgotten.

Maybe it's human nature to dwell on a person's weaknesses. Either real or fabricated, the emphasis is now on Elvis' failures.

Reports of his last years often describe a depressed and reclusive man. That he was in poor health is obvious, but his critics dramatize the overweight Elvis. They continually report his indulgences. The view of many writers seems to be, "If it's not scandalous, it's not interesting." Greed is a powerful motivator, and unfortunately, focusing on the negative side of a celebrity's life seems to be a great money maker.

But what is most sad is that people, whom Elvis knew and took care of, have created their own stories for profit. Even his stepmother, Dee Presley, told a scandalous tale to *The National Enquirer*. Her story was so despicable, and so unfounded, that her own children appeared on television to publicly denounce her. Dee not only hurt herself, Elvis' family and friends, but also her own family and anyone who once considered her a friend. Ursula and Bob Egger remember how warm and kind Dee was when they knew her in the sixties. They can't even imagine that Dee could change so much. But, the nice person Ursula and Bob once knew, sold her dignity away.

Much of Elvis' true character is forgotten. We've lost sight of the man who enjoyed practical jokes and boyish pranks. His generosity and compassion are often overlooked. Few people besides his fans and friends remember he was once voted "One Of the Ten Outstanding Young Men Of America" by the United States Jaycees for his musical accomplishments and for his charitable endeavors. We've forgotten how much Elvis cared about people.

Because Elvis is so often misunderstood today, his fans are even more so. Elvis' critics view his fans as eccentric — why the fascination with that man in the jumpsuit? The answer is very simple. Elvis was more than a performer. He was an inspiration, a man who achieved wealth and fame, but viewed his position as an opportunity to help others. Through their admiration for Elvis, his fans exhibit a youthful idealism in supporting charities. His legacy continues.

"The Best of Elvis" remembers Elvis' finest qualities. It is not a lengthy biography of Elvis Presley. We narrate facts essential for our story. It is not a critical analysis of his music or films. We do not claim our book is a complete accounting of Elvis' acts of kindness. Elvis chose not to publicize many of his charitable contributions or gifts to individuals. Many of his friends and family hold their memories privately. They feel many details should not be shared. Their position is to be respected, for they felt the joy and the pain of Elvis Presley on a very personal level.

We offer a documented, researched story of Elvis' spirit of kindness and generosity. Our stories are a matter of record or were shared with us by those who knew him. Some have been told countless times; others are known to only a few. We chose not to discriminate because Elvis continues to draw new interest and fans. For those well acquainted with the legend, we present new information and a concise package of one topic. Perhaps someone who is not a fan will read this and see Elvis differently. We hope to add credence to a statement made by Elvis' close friend, George Klein. "Think not how Elvis Presley died but remember how Elvis Presley lived."

PART ONE

His Character

—Photo courtesy of Linda Everett.

AN OUSTANDING YOUNG MAN OF AMERICA

*T*here is a dreamer in every man, a yearning for happiness, success, and loving acceptance. No matter how important or prosperous a man may be, no matter his age, his childhood desires merge with his dreams for the future. There is a wish unfulfilled, and a goal that propels him onward.

A man's life is little more than a tapestry of his experiences and emotions. He is a reflection of his past experiences, choices, and dreams combined with his anticipation and hopes as he looks ahead. He is often a contradiction. He will feel one way today and perhaps differently tomorrow. He may say one thing, but do something else. He might outwardly express a desire, yet secretly hope the wish is never fulfilled. He is complex; always changing.

Elvis was such an enigma. He was a mass of contradiction, yet somehow very simple. He was a combination of raw sexuality and traditional values. Once perceived as a threat to all common decency, he was a model of family loyalty and religious faith. He was reputed to be a womanizer; yet, many of his dates contend he read the Bible to them. Considered a wild rock and roller who was a nonconformist in music and dress, he became the ideal soldier, accepting the anonymity of the U.S. Army regulations. He had more fame and fortune than any man could dream of, but at the height of his career, he lost the person he most wanted to share his success with. Some say he never fully recovered from the death of his mother in 1958. The most sought-after man in America, he professed that marriage should be for a lifetime, but he suffered the loss of his wife when she chose another man and lifestyle. His strongest ambition was to become a great actor, but he missed the opportunities to act in award-winning films. He was a perfectionist who was serious about his work; yet, he was prankishly childlike. He was a law-abiding citizen who sought an end to our country's drug problems, while he personally waged an inner battle with prescription drugs. He struggled with his image of handsome youth as middle age approached. He was a symbol of American culture; a hero of supernal proportions. Yet he was gone in an instant—mortal after all.

— To me he was as big as the whole country itself, as big as the whole dream.

—Bruce Springsteen

• • • •

A combination of complexity and innate giftedness made Elvis seem to be different things to different people. He was like the proverbial car accident that is seen by witnesses in divergent ways. A roomful of people might not see the same Elvis. One might see pure masculine sexuality; another would see vulnerability. One might notice his power and control, another his nervousness and insecurity. He was whatever people wished him to be.

For this reason it's difficult to say simply what is the "best" of Elvis. His music may first come to mind—perhaps a gospel song. Maybe it's a performance: a young Elvis at the Tupelo Fair or a mature Elvis in "Aloha From Hawaii." Some people may recall a particular look, gesture, his eyes, or his hands. For others it was his compassion, thoughtfulness, and humble attitude. Possibly, some see a lifetime of achievement.

There's one experience in Elvis' life that may very well describe the best of Elvis, because it encompasses many of these things. On January 16, 1971, Elvis was given what he considered the greatest honor of his life. He was named one of the "Ten Outstanding Young Men of America." This award is an achievement which transcended Elvis' role as an entertainer and recognized his personal qualities.

To select these men, the United States Jaycees nominate men under the age of thirty-six, considered to be exemplary in their fields. Past honorees have included John F. Kennedy, Robert Kennedy, Nelson Rockefeller, Orson Welles, Howard Hughes, and other such notable figures. A panel of distinguished judges, who that year included former President Lyndon Johnson and Memphis business leaders Abe Plough and Kemmons Wilson, pick from the nominees the "Ten Outstanding Young Men Of America." They are selected because they represent "the young ideals that are vital to the growth of America."

Jaycees President, Gordon Thomas, announced the selection. "These men, the best our nation has to offer, first gave the best of themselves to their nation. They have excelled in four main areas of achievement: medical research, government service, personal success and philanthropy, politics and social action."

The Jaycees recognized him as the greatest entertainer of his time but also chose him because of his character. In the awards program the Jaycees said, in part:

> *Throughout his career Elvis has been one of the most civic-minded residents of Memphis, Tennessee, where he has lived since early in his career. Unlike many entertainers, he has intentionally concealed many acts of philanthropy which might have brought him considerable publicity. His personal donations to charity — totaling more than half a million dollars over the last ten years — have been made with little fanfare. His efforts on behalf of projects such as the youth development program of his native Tupelo, Mississippi, have been equally significant though infrequently publicized.*

— Elvis would not let us put in the nomination many things he has done for people in his own industry and for Memphis.

— Frank Taylor
Chairman of the 1971
Jaycees convention

• • • •

*Elvis is noted for his strength of character. His loyalty
to his friends is legendary. His long-standing contract with
his manager consists of a mere handshake.*

Frank Taylor, chairman of the 1971 convention, and other members of the Memphis Jaycees chapter had worked for over two years to bring the annual Jaycees convention and awards ceremony to Memphis. Their success brought the city a tremendous amount of publicity. The NBC television show "Today" broadcast interviews with some of the nominees. Those who orchestrated the convention remember how swiftly the weekend events progressed, and how they moved about with a police escort. They call the experience unforgettable because of the presence of one man: Elvis Presley.

Elvis missed the "Today" show taping and the first day convention activities because he was preparing for a Las Vegas show. Many people doubted he would attend the Jaycees convention at all. Elvis had rarely appeared in person to accept an award. He had not made a public appearance in his hometown since 1961. It was Bill Morris, former Shelby County Sheriff and now Mayor of Shelby County, who convinced his friend Elvis to attend. In other years, Mayor Morris had tried, unsuccessfully, to persuade Elvis to submit a digest of his accomplishments to the Jaycees, the first step in the nomination process. Elvis reluctantly gave his permission to the nomination in 1970.

He felt the other recipients had accomplished far more than he had. These men were finding cures for cancer, organizing communities, and building business empires. They were all educated. Elvis saw himself as just an entertainer.

Elvis Aaron Presley, 35—Musician/Entertainer—Memphis, Tennessee.

The success of Elvis Aaron Presley is a phenomenon of the entertainment world. Elvis is one of the most well known and prolific entertainers in the Nation. Fifty-one of his single records have won Gold Record awards for sales of more than one million records. Fourteen of his albums have won Gold Album awards. Over 200 million of his recordings have been sold around the world. He has sung and acted in 32 major motion pictures. Elvis performs before sell out crowds wherever he appears.

Elvis began his professional career with the Louisiana Hayride. In late 1955 his record, "That's All Right Mama," brought him national attention. Four television appearances with Tommy and Jimmy Dorsey, one with Milton Berle and four with Ed Sullivan made him a national entertainment figure.

Excerpt from the Jaycees Awards Program.

—Courtesy of Barbara McAlpin

Elvis' record breaking entry into the music industry resulted in the creation of the first Gold Album award in 1957 when, for the first time, an album sold more than one million copies. The award presented to him read: "First Album to Sell One Million Copies — One of the Greatest Achievements in this History of the Record Industry.—1957."

In 1969 he won three gold records and albums: "His Hand in Mine", "In The Ghetto", and "Elvis TV Special". His television special the same year, demonstrated his remarkable talent, tradition and flair that continues to capture the imagination of millions.

Elvis has won multiple honors from virtually every entertainment industry group. His singing has brought 17 Broadcast Music Awards for individual songs. Elvis possesses a talent which spans decades and continents. He is a favorite of music lovers of all ages in the United States and around the world.

Despite the fact that he has never been in the United Kingdom, he has been Great Britain's leading recording artist for 14 years. Even in nations as remote as South Africa, he is well known. During 1960 a total of 10 million of his records were sold in South Africa.

The *Guinness Book of World Records* reported that Elvis had sold by January, 1965, total global sales of over 110,000,000 discs. His current sales record is more than 200,000,000.

Throughout his career Elvis has been one of the most civic-minded residents of Memphis, Tennessee, where he has lived since early in his career. Unlike many entertainers, he has intentionally concealed many acts of philanthropy which might have brought him considerable publicity. His personal donations to charity—totaling more than half a million dollars over the last 10 years—have been made with little fanfare. His efforts in behalf of projects such as the youth development program of his native Tupelo, Mississippi, have been equally significant though infrequently publicized.

Elvis is noted for his strength of character. His loyalty to his friends is legendary. His long-standing contract with his manager consists of a mere handshake.

Elvis is married. He and his wife, Priscilla Ann have one daughter, Lisa Marie, age two and a half. They reside in Memphis, maintain a home in California.

Being in the presence of these confident, professional men genuinely honored Elvis. The other honorees accepted Elvis as an equal and did not fawn over him. Elvis appreciated that, and remarked again and again how impressed he was with them. He was, for one of the few moments in his life, relaxed and unguarded because the pressure was shared by the other honorees; they were all in the spotlight. During private Jaycees functions Elvis asked his bodyguards not to interfere with those who wanted to talk to him. Ron Ziegler, a fellow honoree who was President Nixon's press secretary, remembers: "Elvis wanted to reach out and talk to someone outside of his entourage. He was withdrawn and shy but hardly dull or limited. All of us were sort of moved by him."

The Jaycees convention delegates, however, were star-struck. Harold Sterling, co-chairman of the convention, remembers the first event Elvis attended—the prayer breakfast at the Rivermont Hotel. "Everyone was seated for the breakfast, the honorees at tables among the guests. I looked around and panicked . . . Elvis was not there. I rode the freight elevator to his floor and found Priscilla and his bodyguards standing there, patiently waiting. It seems Elvis was missing a cuff link and had gone back to the room to change. Priscilla laughed, 'I'm so glad it happened to him. If one of us had been late he never would have let us hear the end of it. You know his motto: speed and efficiency.'"

"We stood and talked for a few moments, then saw him start down the hall. We got in the elevator, and Elvis stepped in. His hair was long, jet black. He was wearing a brown fur suit with a 'Johnny Cash' type (high) collar and a tuxedo shirt with frills. Jewels on the nose piece of his sunglasses formed EP. He had rings on all four fingers of both hands and they were covered with diamonds. He was smoking a very thin, long cigar. I was overwhelmed. I'm not sure what I expected but I didn't expect him to look like this. This was a breakfast!

For the first time he was being placed on the level with achievers in realms other than entertainment and for the first time Elvis felt he was being accepted like a true professional. He really felt like a human being.

—Frank Taylor

• • • •

Watch out for Elvis Presley should he decide to enter politics. They would have to regroup their forces.

—George Bush
Then Ambassador to the United
Nations and the keynote speaker
for the Jaycees luncheon,
January 16, 1971

• • • •

"We rode the elevator downstairs and entered the service corridor. I stepped into the meeting room while Elvis continued walking down the corridor toward the opposite door. I looked around the room and saw fifteen hundred people talking and eating. It was very ordinary, a lot of chatter and the noises of dishes clinking together. And then, Elvis walked into the room. Suddenly, it was very quiet and you could feel the electricity. These were not teen-agers; they were all thirty- to forty-year-olds attending a convention. They rushed to him for his autograph. I've never seen anyone have that affect on people."

As Elvis and Priscilla sat down, they were surrounded by photographers. Elvis allowed a couple of pictures but then ordered his security men to clear the area of newsmen and photographers. He insisted on privacy because he didn't want to overshadow the other honorees.

In a closed meeting following the breakfast, members of the Jaycees questioned the young men. To encourage them to speak candidly, the press were not allowed to attend. Elvis was asked if he felt today's music had an adverse affect on young people. He replied "Yes, I don't go along with music advocating drugs and desecration of the flag. I think an entertainer is for entertaining and to make people happy." When asked what career he would have chosen if he had not become an entertainer, Elvis answered, "I would have liked to have gone into law enforcement."

All of the men were asked if they made a religious commitment before undertaking their life's work. The majority of the men didn't speak of strong religious beliefs. But Elvis was different. He did not express a need for an organized church, but felt religion was very important in his life. He had called on God many times for strength.

Throughout the day, Elvis was approached by his fans. After the Saturday rehearsal for the awards ceremony, he walked out of

Ellis Auditorium toward his car. Instinctively, his bodyguards locked arms, and surrounded him. Just as quickly, crowds of people, including some Jaycees, rushed toward him, clutching at him. Ron Ziegler, after seeing the Memphis Mafia (the name given to Elvis' bodyguards) in action told him, "You know, you use the same strategy and tactics we use to protect the President."

Elvis' tight security was finely tuned during these events. Even the press were confused about his plans for the afternoon; they did not know Elvis was hosting a cocktail party at Graceland for the honorees, their host couples, and Jaycees officers.

Elvis personally greeted his guests, and as each nominee entered his home, Elvis presented him with an expensive watch. He had designed the watches with his name, "Elvis Presley," written around the face. Unfortunately, he mistakenly gave a watch to a local Jaycees officer, confusing him for an honoree. Though the recipient knew the gift was given in error, Elvis refused to embarrass the man by asking for the watch. Instead, he had another made for the nominee who didn't receive one.

The party was held in the trophy room. Frank Taylor remembers how impressive the room was. "It was hard for me to believe, looking upon gold records, upon gold records. It was just unbelievable to see all of the gold and platinum."

Elvis was a gracious host, but a little ill at ease. He confided in Harold Sterling. "Elvis had recently been named the father in a paternity suit, and there had been a lot of publicity. He was really embarrassed. He pulled me aside and told me he wished it (the story) hadn't happened and hoped it wouldn't put a damper on the events. Of course nothing could dampen our enthusiasm." Elvis was later found innocent of the charge.

Elvis visited with his guests, talking to them in small groups. Mary Taylor (the chairman's wife) remembers, "I never thought I

I remember when I went to Graceland to plan the cocktail party. Elvis was out of town but I met with Marty Lacker. The home was so impressive, very glitzy and decorated in red and black. There were two great Danes in the house and Lisa, who was about four years old, was playing with them.

—Harold Sterling

• • • •

Elvis and Priscilla at the prayer breakfast.

was in awe of him, but being in his presence I was very nervous and excited. I just couldn't believe I was really there, standing and talking to Elvis."

Another member of the Jaycees talked with Elvis about his movies. Not holding anything back, he told Elvis he thought his films were terrible. Elvis politely replied, "I know it. They were awful. I couldn't stand them but I had no choice. The Colonel obligated me to do them."

From Graceland, the party moved to the Four Flames Restaurant on Poplar Avenue for dinner. Elvis provided limousines and

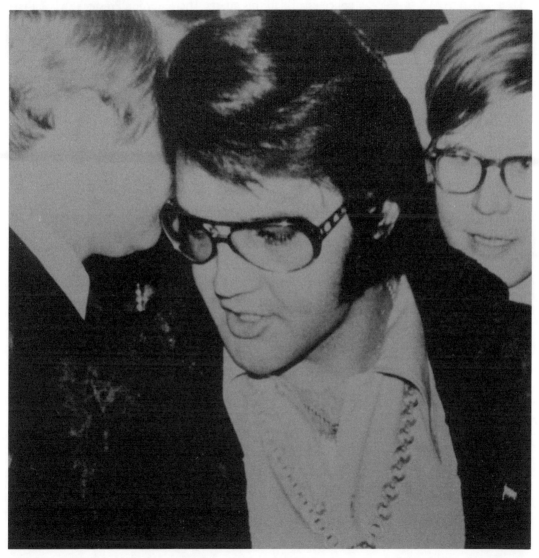

—Photo courtesy of Linda Everett.

police escorts for his guests. There, Vernon Presley (Elvis' father) invited everyone to be their guests in Las Vegas. He was very proud of Elvis and the award he was about to receive.

The awards ceremony was held later that night at Ellis Auditorium. Though tickets were available for five thousand people, only two thousand attended, probably because people didn't believe Elvis would appear.

As a way of introduction, the U.S. Jaycees compiled a three or four minute film clip for each of the honorees detailing their accomplishments. The film was shown on a large screen behind the stage, and ended with a spotlight shone on the honoree who stood at the top of the stairs. The honoree would walk to the podium, accept his award, and make a speech.

I shall always remember a line that Elvis used to quote from "Patton." In it General George S. Patton says, "All glory is fleeting." Elvis knew that.

—Linda Thompson

• • • •

The nominees were seated in the order they were to receive their award; Elvis was to receive his last. Frank Taylor noticed Elvis was shifting in his chair, sweating profusely. When Frank asked him what was wrong, Elvis replied, "I'm scared to death. I've never done anything like this before. I'm like this all the time, before every show, but not as bad as this." Ironically, Elvis, who had performed before enormous crowds, was more nervous than any of the other honorees. Frank was worried that he wouldn't be able calm him. But, somehow, Elvis found the strength to go on.

Harold Sterling described the excitement when the spotlight shone on Elvis. "Elvis stood at the top of the stairs and the crowd went crazy. He had a way of being very provocative—the way he moved, held himself, or turned his head—that was a turn-on to both men and women. The other men had dressed in conservative tuxedos and when the lights flashed on them they stood very erect. Not Elvis. He wore a high fashion, black tuxedo. When the light came on him his stance was provocative. He shone on stage and the people loved him." Elvis walked to the podium and nervously spoke about his childhood.

*I read comic books and I was the hero of the comic book. I
saw movies and I was the hero of the movie. So every dream
that I ever dreamed has come true a hundred times. . . .*
   And . . . these gentlemen here,

He gestured to the other winners and choked. His eyes filled with tears.

*See, these are the type people who care. They're dedicated.
You realize, they might be building the Kingdom of Heaven
right here. It's not too far-fetched to believe that.*
   *I'd like to say that I learned, very early in life that, without
a song the day would never end, without a song, a man ain't
got a friend, without a song, the road would never bend,
without a song, so I'll keep singing the song.*

After the ceremony, Elvis invited the honorees and Jaycees officers to his hotel suite. Elvis and his guests were relaxed and comfortable. Suddenly, as if someone had snapped a finger, the Memphis Mafia jumped up. The guests were escorted to the door. Elvis was on his way back to Vegas, back to his own world.

Later that year, Frank Taylor edited the film footage of the convention and produced a documentary. He gave a copy of the film to each of the honorees as a remembrance of the events. Elvis asked for two, one for Graceland and one for his California home.

The Jaycees award is a silver statue in the shape of two hands, outstretched, and touching each other. Its inscription reads, "Hope of mankind lies in the hands of youth and action." Today the statue is on display in the trophy room at Graceland. Visitors notice the scratches and scuff marks on it and ask, why? Because Elvis carried the statue on every tour, to every place he went. It was placed next to his bed, within his reach until his death.

*When Elvis gave his speech, he
spoke of his humble beginnings
and how grateful he was. It was
very short but it was one of the
most sincere talks I've ever heard.*
   —Harold Sterling

• • • •

—Elvis with fellow honorees after
the awards ceremony.
   —Photo courtesy of Graceland.

· C H A P T E R · II ·

THE IMAGE
IS ONE THING

*E*lvis once said, "I can never forget the longing to be someone. I guess if you're poor, you always think bigger and want more than those who have everything when they are born. We didn't. So our dreams and ambitions could be much greater because we had so much further to go than anyone else."

Raised in poverty, Elvis was the archetypical hero who rose almost overnight to unprecedented wealth and fame. Within three years after his high school graduation he was a millionaire, credited with changing the world of music. He was called the "King of Rock and Roll," a role he was completely unprepared for. He was raised to expect an ordinary, hard-working life. Due to opportunity or fate, Elvis' life had been transformed.

Many people have said that fame never really changed him. He was the same personality at forty-two as at twenty. Many others have said fame changed everything about him. Both points of view are accurate. Elvis kept many of the values of his childhood: concern for others, appreciation for those who helped him, a sense of humor, and a strong belief in God. What changed most about Elvis was his lifestyle.

Elvis compensated for celebrity by inventing a new world. Night became day because he found greater freedom while most people slept. He indulged in his childhood fantasies with big and

The most fun I had in Hollywood was a visit to the Long Beach amusement park when I won eight teddy bears before I had to quit because so many kids followed me.
—Elvis

• • • •

expensive toys. He rented amusement parks or roller skating rinks for himself and several hundred of his friends. If he wanted to ride motorcycles he bought them for everyone around him. When he wanted to play football, he started his own team, furnished all of the equipment, and rented the Whitehaven High School stadium.

His income allowed him to do what he liked, and Elvis liked to have fun. On the movie sets he was known as a practical joker. He would rig a bucket of water over the door so that it would spill on the first person to come through. He would start pie throwing fights or set off firecrackers at unexpected moments. Once, while performing at the Las Vegas Hilton, he fired a water pistol at his band and the front row audience. And he and his orchestra leader, Joe Guercio, had a round of one-upmanship. Joe surrendered when Elvis had a truck load of marbles delivered to his house. No one knew what to expect when Elvis was around.

Richard Davis, Elvis' valet and friend for many years, was in Hawaii with him when Elvis did the unthinkable. They were staying on the top floor of the Illikai Hotel in Waikiki during the filming of "Paradise Hawaiian Style." It was a slow day and they entertained themselves for a while by sailing 45 rpm records out of the window into the ocean. Eventually they became bored and went across the hallway to the other side of the hotel. Richard was standing at the window when Elvis asked, "What are you looking at?"

"Well, I'm looking at limousines, Rolls Royces, pretty ladies in their evening gowns, and men in their tuxedos," Richard answered.

"They ain't so hot," said Elvis as he walked over to the dresser drawer and pulled out a stack of bills.

"No, you're not going to."

"Watch me," Elvis responded, as he threw five thousand dollars in ten and twenty dollar bills, out of the window.

When Elvis became famous, he changed in some ways, but not others. He rode around in Rolls Royce cars and could buy all the fancy clothes he wanted, whenever he wanted them and however much they cost. But deep down he was still the same old boy I'd known in Memphis. He'd still ask me what I thought of his clothes and ask me to play touch football.

—Johnny Burnette/musician

• • • •

"What did you do that for?" Richard asked.

As the ladies and men, all in their finery, dived into the fountain after that money, Elvis answered, "See, they ain't high class."

Elvis wasn't impressed with status. Early in his career he had to learn to be treated as a celebrity. At some of the Graceland parties Elvis would enter a room and suddenly the laughter and talking would stop. All eyes would focus on him, waiting for his next move. He would respond with a joke, "What are you looking at me for? I didn't do anything."

Though he awed virtually everyone he met, he knew how to put people at ease. His dentist, Dr. Hoffman, remembers, "When Elvis talked to my wife he spoke to her as if no one else existed. When he talked with me he insisted on using the title, *doctor*, saying, 'Well, you went to school, got yourself an education, and you're entitled to respect.'"

Elvis realized his power over people and he tried to accommodate them. The word most often used to describe Elvis by the people who knew him is *humble*. Although his name was the most recognized in the world, he didn't act as if he expected everyone to know who he was. He would walk up to someone, extend his hand warmly and say, "Hi. I'm Elvis Presley."

Those few words left a compelling impression. Joe Kent was a young boy when he met Elvis. One evening his mother told him to bathe because she had a date with Elvis and he was coming to pick her up. Joe thought it was an ingenious ploy to get him into the bath tub. He really didn't believe his mother until he saw the Stutz Blackhawk pull into the driveway. When Joe answered the door, Elvis reached out and tousled Joe's hair as he introduced himself. Joe laughs as he remembers how much time his mother had spent combing it. Before leaving for the evening, Elvis took Joe out to the driveway and showed him his car.

Elvis was the guy they started out to hate and ended up loving. Around the studio he soon endeared himself to most of his fellow workers by calling himself "Elvis Pretzel"—the name the folks who didn't like him invented. I remember, one technician admitted to me, 'You know, me and the boys were all ready to hate this Presley. We tried hard to, but gotta admit we even look forward to him coming on the set now. He's just like one of us.'

—Charles O'Curran/song and dance director

•   •   •   •

Joe's memories of that night are vivid. He remembers how friendly Elvis was. He was impressed with Elvis' appearance. Elvis was the cleanest man he had ever met. Most of the men he had been around were working class and usually had grease under their fingernails. Elvis' hands were perfectly manicured. He remembers the Stutz with the gold-plated gear shift and the floormats with the initials EP. Most of all, he remembers that Elvis spent time with him and seemed interested in what he had to say.

It wasn't unusual for Elvis to spend a few moments with someone he had just met. Once, Elvis and Colonel Parker were waiting to board a plane. Elvis disappeared, and the Colonel couldn't find him. He searched desperately, knowing their plane would soon be ready for takeoff. Finally, he saw him. Elvis was pitching pennies with a taxi driver outside of the terminal.

Elvis had a knack for making each person feel special, however brief their encounter. A newspaper describes Elvis' return from Germany. "One in the small sea of faces pressed against the iron barrier waiting for a glimpse of Elvis Presley belonged to a girl of about twenty, a little short and plump, and wearing glasses. The young woman pressed her face tightly against the bars and reached out a hand. The young man smiled her a gentle smile, took her hand briefly in his, and passed on. For a second her eyes followed him. Then she closed her eyes, pressed her lips tightly together, and stood trembling. For maybe half a minute she stood like that, then she began to cry."

Elvis didn't single out beautiful girls when he gave out kisses. He often chose someone very ordinary and plain who most likely did not receive a lot of male attention. He knew a small gesture would affect such a girl deeply. For a moment, at least, she would feel beautiful and loved.

—Photo courtesy of Linda Everett

Elvis gave as much of himself as one could possibly give to people. His charm was natural and sincere. He didn't put on an act but, in a sense, he was always "on stage," trying to live up to his image. In public, he was immaculately groomed because he was expected to look like a star. He was conscious of his every word, knowing that if he expressed anger or unusual opinions he could be quoted in the next news story.

Because Elvis fulfilled his role so well, few could see beyond the image of "ELVIS!" the star. But he didn't always enjoy being in the limelight. At home, or with his friends, he wanted to relax and be just "one of the guys." He told his friends he rarely had a chance to act like a normal human being.

Elvis knew that a lot of the people who hung around Graceland were there to enjoy the benefits of his fame. He had lost the simplicity of choosing friends that is so often taken for granted in ordinary life. Eddie Fadal, who shared a close friendship with Elvis since 1956, said, "He was warm, sensitive, honest, and deeply believed everyone is the same. He learned the hard way that everyone is not trustworthy, especially some of those who surrounded him, and used him." Elvis was vulnerable.

He's naturally kind and thoughtful and good. Best of all, in spite of his huge success, he's unassuming.

—Connie Francis

• • • •

Elvis found it difficult to openly discourage those who were not sincere. Instead, he treated those in his inner circle as they treated him. Those who responded to Elvis as a person were usually treated with respect. Others, who played up to him and treated him like a star, usually had more demands placed on them. He once said, "I can find eight people to jump up and get me a Coke, but I have very few friends."

With so many willing to wait on him, Elvis was sometimes overbearing. Some people who knew him have said that everything centered around Elvis' enjoyment. When he rented a theater, he would demand that the movie be stopped if he didn't like it, even if everyone else was enjoying the film. He wouldn't think twice about calling someone at four in the morning, even if he knew the person had to get up for work in the next few hours. But few people complained because they were so pleased to get a call from him.

Other friends have said Elvis was always concerned about their wishes before his own. If he was demanding, they wonder, how was Elvis being treated? Maybe those around him were more interested in Elvis' position than his friendship. And now, they say, so many incidents are distorted. One friend remembers kidding about the clouds, joking that he had moved them. She said they would roll over laughing. Now, it's been written the he believed that he could psychically move clouds at will. "It's a complete untruth."

Perhaps too much was expected of him. His closest friends learned to shield him from the endless number of people who wanted to meet him, touch him, and talk to him. Some of these people wanted more from Elvis than a handshake and greeting. He was approached for money to start businesses, fund religious organizations, and even heal the sick. Although Elvis was very compassionate—when he heard of someone's troubles he felt their pain—the constant demands became a terrible burden.

While in the Army Elvis remarked, "I have a lot more personal freedom than I had before. Of course I have to do what I'm told during the day, or whenever I'm on duty, but outside of my duty hours I am free to do whatever I like. Before, I was protected wherever I went. Security police were hired to guard my hotel and I could never go to a public place in case I got mobbed. I guess those things had to be done. But that kind of protection can get isolating. After a time it makes a guy feel pretty lonely."

Yea, I know, it's like everything is supposedly taboo because people are afraid they will say something that will upset you or make you feel bad, so they tell you something that isn't true.

—Elvis
speaking to Glen Campbell

• • • •

When Elvis resumed his career after being discharged from the Army, he never again had that freedom. He missed a simpler existence. His birthplace, Tupelo, Mississippi, was often in his thoughts, reminding him of another time, when no one was better than anyone else, when everyone struggled to get by. In 1961 Elvis was asked if he always felt Memphis was home. He responded, "Yes, sir, I like to work in California but when a picture is over I look forward to getting out of there and coming back home, and also I'm right near Tupelo. I know a lot of people down there. The same old crowd I was raised up with is still there, living in the same houses."

One of his friends from Tupelo was Janelle McComb. Throughout his life she remained loyal. Her life was still ordinary and she treated Elvis like anyone else. She often brought him things from the country, a bushel of peas or some remembrance of home. Although proud of him, she loved him for who he was and not for his success. He was just Elvis, not the icon living behind the gates of Graceland. He was someone she had known all of her life, a real person with dreams and fears. For Elvis, she and others like her were a tie to the real world. He missed that contact.

Janelle remembers the man. The Elvis she knew sent her flowers while she was in the hospital. The name of her favorite song, told to Elvis in a conversation long ago, was written on the card. She reminisces about visiting Graceland and pulling her shoes off as she entered the house. Beyond the stone wall it was a home where she was made to feel comfortable. She remembers Elvis gently cupping her face with his hands, and asking her how she was. Janelle recalls presenting Elvis with the poem, "The Priceless Gift," which she had written for Elvis as a present for his daughter, Lisa Marie. As Elvis read the poem, tears streamed down his cheeks. He signed Janelle's copy but his tears fell on the paper, smearing his name.

A big part of the problem was that people had put him in a place he couldn't live up to. They just didn't understand that he wasn't a god, he was a man. He carried a very heavy burden.

—Priscilla Presley

• • • •

"Mrs. McComb," Elvis said, "I've ruined your copy."

Janelle replied, "No Elvis, someday those tears will be priceless."

Years later Janelle wrote . . .

He lives in my own life because he allowed me to share my talent with him and, in so doing, added a new dimension to the quality of loyalty within me that I treasure. He lives because when he was pleased with my bit of talent he would look at me and say in that beautiful resonant voice, 'Mrs. McComb, you are really sump'n.' He lives within me because in knowing him I came to the realization that all the wealth in the world can't buy a friend or pay for the loss of one."

—Photo courtesy of Linda Everett

MY KIND OF MUSIC

*E*very year nearly 700,000 people tour Graceland. Many are curiosity seekers, not Elvis' fans. Regardless of personal feelings toward Elvis, one part of the tour impresses everyone who passes through. Though the trophy room houses only a small number of Elvis' awards, honors, and memorabilia from his twenty-three year career, it contains more than anyone can imagine being achieved in a lifetime.

In the "hall of gold," gold and platinum records are displayed on the walls along the entire forty-foot length of the room—an incredible accomplishment for an entertainer. Because Elvis' impact on the music industry was so phenomenal, RCA created the gold record award in 1956 when his first recording on their label, "Heartbreak Hotel," reached one million sales.

Elvis received well over one hundred and fifty gold records—no one is sure of the exact number—and many platinum records. Virtually everything he sang turned gold. In 1961, just five years after receiving his first gold award, RCA presented Elvis with an award recognizing seventy-five million in sales. Considering two of those years were spent in the Army far from a recording studio, this feat was extraordinary. No other entertainer has approached Elvis in record sales.

A part of this success may be attributed to Elvis' unprecedented ability to reach all audiences. His records not only made it to the number one position on the pop charts, but they also reached

Sometimes when I walk into a room at home and see all those gold records hanging around the walls, I think they must belong to another person, not me, I just can't believe that it's me.

—Elvis

• • • •

the number one mark in rhythm and blues, easy listening, and country and western. Unlike many performers who are proficient at one type of music, Elvis was a master of different forms. He could sing rock and roll with the same adeptness as country, rhythm and blues, or gospel, and he could incorporate these styles into any type of recording. The effect was a versatility so

Elvis receiving the Bing Crosby Award in 1971 from the National Academy of Recording Arts and Sciences.

—Photo courtesy of the Jerry Hopkins Collection, Memphis State University

unique it was not easy to categorize. Elvis captured awards in many types of music.

Elvis was nominated for the Grammy Award, the most coveted award in the music industry, on sixteen different occasions. He won this prestigious award three times; ironically, Elvis won in the inspirational music category, not for his popular music. But because Elvis loved sacred music above all others, these awards were particularly gratifying to him.

From the first visit to the Assembly of God Church in East Tupelo with his mother and father, religion was a constant influence. Their faith was uncomplicated by theological dogma. All men were sinners who could only be redeemed by accepting God's presence in their lives. They were "saved" by a forgiving God, often in a spirit of their emotional fervor. The congregation was a musical church; singing rhythmic gospel hymns was a form of prayer. Those who didn't understand their belief dismissed them as "holy rollers."

Elvis listened to his family and neighbors sing gospel hymns at nearly every church gathering. At Sunday services the congregation was led in song by Reverend Frank Smith, who played guitar. During evangelical revival meetings he heard the enthusiastic congregation sing gospel music. He watched revival preachers shout, jump around on stage, and urge their congregation to a joyous ecstasy. Elvis saw how a preacher could move a crowd to focus on him and his message.

In Memphis, Elvis attended the First Assembly of God Church, which was then located at 1084 McLemore. The Presleys did not always attend together and sometimes Elvis went alone, riding the church bus from his home downtown to the church on the south side of town. Elvis attended Sunday School and sang in the church choir. The famed gospel quartet, the Blackwood Brothers, joined the church in 1950 and Elvis became friends with the family.

Elvis also visited the East Trigg Baptist Church, where the Reverend Harper Brewster preached. A well-known songwriter, Reverend Brewster combined the sacred message in his gospel compositions with a blues influence. The Reverend and most of his congregation were black. Through his radio show on WDIA, "Old Camp Meeting Of The Air," he encouraged whites to participate in the singing and to come to his Sunday night services. Years later Reverend Brewster praised Elvis for transcending the racial barriers of the era, because of his love for music.

Elvis' voice agreed with the thought of Calvary.
—Reverend Harper Brewster

• • • •

Elvis also attended gospel concerts at Ellis Auditorium in Memphis each month. When his friends, the Blackwood Brothers, performed at these shows, Elvis would visit them backstage. He became friends with J.D. Sumner, a bass singer who joined the Blackwood Brothers in 1954. One month, after he failed to attend the gospel "sings," J.D. asked him where he had been. Elvis explained that he didn't have any money for admission. J.D. said he didn't need any money; from then on to come to the back door and he would let him in for free. J.D. jokes that it wasn't too much longer before Elvis was letting him in the back door of his shows.

Elvis dreamed of becoming a professional gospel singer. He studied the famous gospel performers and asked them questions backstage. Sometimes when they rehearsed, Elvis sang with them. In 1954 he auditioned for the Songfellows, a youth group associated with the Blackwood Brothers. Stories vary as to why he did not join the group. At any rate, if not for a quick turn of events with Sun Studios, Elvis might have had another career.

In a sense, he never gave up on the dream of singing gospel music. He wanted a choir sound in his own recordings. When he began recording for RCA in 1956, he asked the Jordanaires, another of his favorite gospel quartets, to sing with him. He had heard them in Memphis in 1954, and told them, "If I ever have a recording contract, I want you guys to sing back-up for me." He lived up to his word. They sang backing vocals on several of his hit recordings.

The year 1956 was pivotal for Elvis. A sudden celebrity, much of the media attention was not pleasant for him. He was under attack by many for what they called vulgar, indecent performances. He turned to gospel music. A scene from the documentary video, "Elvis 56" (from still photographs by Alfred Wertheimer), illustrates this. Elvis was at the RCA studios in New York rehearsing before his appearance on "The Steve Allen Show." Mr. Allen had made it clear he intended to humiliate Elvis on national television. That day in the studio, Elvis consoled himself at the piano, playing and singing a gospel song.

Ed Sullivan refused to have Elvis on his show until he realized how enormous Elvis' popularity was. He gave in and had Elvis appear on three shows. On the third and final appearance Sullivan showed Elvis only from the waist up, because he had received complaints about Elvis from television viewers.

With an entire nation anxious about Elvis' influence, he offered a stunning rendition of "Peace in the Valley." The audience was caught completely off guard and loved it. The last thing Elvis' critics expected was a gospel song. How could parents complain about their daughters watching this young man if he sang a well-known hymn? Ed Sullivan then told the audience Elvis was a fine, decent, young boy, and having him on the show was one of the best experiences he had had with a big name entertainer. It was a turning point for Elvis. The older generation began to think of him as an entertainer and less as a threat to decency.

It was a daring move for a rock and roll star to sing gospel on a national television show. Yet his performance succeeded because of his sincerity; his religious passion came through clearly. After the show, RCA received more demands for sacred recordings. Elvis and the Jordanaires recorded his first gospel EP, (an extended play disc of four songs) also called "Peace In The Valley."

Elvis began all of his recording sessions singing gospel music with the quartet. It was his way of preparing himself. D.J. Fontana, his drummer, remembers, "One thing he loved to do was sit around and sing gospel. We had more trouble with that than anything when we went to Hollywood to record for those movies. The first thing Elvis would want to do would be to play gospel music. We'd play for hours and the movie people would get upset. It was all money to them. They were afraid to say anything to Elvis, so they'd come over to us and beg us to stop. But I told one of those people, 'He's the guy who's paying me. If he wants to sing gospel all day long, I'll play it.'" When Elvis heard of the complaints, he walked out of the studio, visibly angry. The next day he returned to work and the management gave in to his needs. Elvis would sing gospel whenever he liked.

Elvis regretted his fame had become so great he could no longer go to church for fear of being mobbed. The conflict between his religion and his career was never fully resolved. His talent, he felt, was a gift from God. Yet, his fame pulled him from his family and his church. His life was filled with the temptations he was taught to avoid, and he struggled with guilt when he could not resist. He continued to read the Bible as he grew older but also studied other religions and philosophies. He wanted to know why he was chosen to be who he was.

Elvis recorded his first gospel long-play album, "His Hand In Mine," in 1960, two years after his mother's death. He was still mourning her. Many of the songs in this album speak of death and the hope of everlasting life: "If We Never Meet Again (This

In all the years I traveled and worked with Elvis I never heard him raise his voice to anyone except one time.

—Gordon Stoker/member of the Jordanaires

• • • •

Side Of Heaven)," "Milky White Way" ("I'm gonna tell my mother 'howdy' when I get home,") and "Known Only To Him."

When Elvis felt discouraged by his career, he turned to gospel music. He was his own worst critic and judged many of his performances in his movies and soundtrack recordings as sub-par, as shallow. They were not creatively satisfactory to him. But he fulfilled his lucrative contracts. In 1966 and 1967, when he was recording movie soundtracks that he disliked, he recorded the gospel music album, "How Great Thou Art." He won his first Grammy for that album in 1967.

Occasionally, he slipped a gospel performance into one of his movies. During the film, "The Trouble With Girls," Elvis sang "Swing Low Sweet Chariot," with the Jordanaires and it was a highlight of the film. Elvis performed "Let Us Pray," with the Blossoms vocal group at the end of the movie, "Change of Habit."

When Elvis began his Las Vegas shows in 1969, he asked the Jordanaires to return to the stage with him. But they elected to stay in Nashville, and opted to sing with Elvis whenever he recorded there.

Instead, Elvis brought several of his friends in gospel out to Las Vegas. His confidante and helper on stage, Charlie Hodge, joined Elvis after singing with many gospel groups. Soprano Kathy Westmoreland, who joined him in 1971, had grown up with gospel music; her father directed gospel choirs. The Sweet Inspirations, a black vocalist trio, had performed as a gospel group before backing Elvis. The Imperials were a quartet who recorded "How Great Thou Art" with Elvis. When the Imperials could not tour with Elvis in 1971, he asked his friend J.D. Sumner and his group The Stamps to join him. J.D. and The Stamps sang backing vocals for Elvis until his death.

Kathy Westmoreland, in her book, *Elvis and Kathy*, wrote of his commitment to gospel music. Elvis decided to put a gospel song in

I remember my first meeting with Elvis, when I presented him with his first British-earned Gold Disc for "It's Now or Never" in 1960. Elvis said, "Gee, isn't it fabulous?" And then he did something quite unexpected—I knew he already had thirty-four Gold Discs—he danced around the set clutching the latest trophy in his hands and showing it to everyone—artists, technicians and studio hands. Even as we chatted he wouldn't put it aside or give it to someone else to take to his dressing room.

—Jimmy Savile/British
music personality

● ● ● ●

—Photo courtesy of Linda Everett

his Las Vegas show. In typical Elvis fashion, he decided it had to be done immediately—in that night's performance. He gathered the other vocalists for a quick rehearsal of "How Great Thou Art." Singing a sacred song in Las Vegas was, at the very least, risky. It didn't fit the image. But the audience loved the song and gave the performers a standing ovation. Elvis said, "See, I knew they'd like our kind of music." From that point on, gospel became a regular part of his shows.

In nervous moments before a performance, when Elvis felt the need to pray, he would take the quartet aside and he, J.D., and The Stamps would quietly perform an inspirational number for their own benefit. They sang gospel in bathrooms and hallways across America. It was only after these sessions that he felt comfortable enough to go on. Even in the early morning hours after a concert, Elvis and the group would gather around a piano and sing their favorite hymns. The singing was relaxing, a form of meditation. Gospel singing was Elvis' way of worship.

No matter how famous Elvis became, he always looked up to gospel singers. He wanted to share their talent with his audiences. In many concerts, Elvis gave his vocalists the stage to perform a favorite hymn. He would quietly stand aside with his head bowed, and listen intently. One of J.D.'s fondest memories is of a concert in Asheville, North Carolina, when Elvis told the audience, "This man has never let me down. I never thought I'd get to be on his stage. J.D., it's a privilege to share your stage. I heard this man singing when I was fourteen years old and I never thought I'd get to sing on his stage."

Shaun Nielsen, a tenor singer, then with the Statesmen quartet attended one of Elvis' shows. Elvis introduced him to the audience. Shaun recalls the thrill when "the biggest entertainer in the world took the time to introduce me." Soon Shaun was part of the show, singing backing tenor and duets with Elvis.

Elvis loved gospel music. He was raised on it. And he really knew what he was talking about. He was singing gospel all the time, almost anything he did had that flavor anyhow. At least I heard it. You can't get away from what your roots are.

—Cissy Houston/Singer with the Sweet Inspirations

• • • •

J.D. has said, "He drew in thousands of people and witnessed to them in a way by having us sing some gospel, having Kathy sing "My Heavenly Father," Sherril (Shaun) sing "Walk With Me," calling us out to sing "Sweet, Sweet Spirit." He knew what he was and how powerful he was. When he sang "How Great Thou Art," he did it with such power and feeling that I know it affected people tremendously."

Benefit Concerts and Charities

—Photo courtesy of Bill Burk.

Elvis with the King and Queen of Cotton at the Memphis Cotton Carnival, 1956.

    —Photo courtesy of Linda Everett.

· C H A P T E R · IV ·

HOMECOMING

Our memories of Elvis are of a confident, successful performer. It is sometimes difficult to picture the Elvis of 1954 who nervously walked into Sam Phillips' Memphis Recording Service with the story of making a record for his mother. It's hard to imagine the release of his first hit song, "That's All Right Mama," and the swift course of events that followed. Sam had asked two young musicians, Scotty Moore and Bill Black, to practice with the unpolished singer. Together, they unwittingly created the rock and roll sound by fooling with blues and country and western songs. Their first shows were simple. They performed on the back of a flatbed truck for the grand opening of the Katz Drug Store in Memphis, at small nightclubs around town, and at their first "big" concert at the Overton Park Shell.

Just one month after "That's All Right Mama" hit the charts, Elvis participated in the Kennedy Veterans Hospital's benefit show, sponsored by the B'nai B'rith Society. It was not the first time he had performed at the hospital. As a boy Elvis visited patients, sometimes bringing his guitar and entertaining them, perhaps dreaming of playing to a wider audience.

Although Elvis' dream was becoming a reality in Memphis, he faced the challenge of spreading his popularity to other areas of the country. In November 1954, Elvis earned one of his first big breaks, a contract to appear on the "Louisiana Hayride" radio show broadcast by KWKH in Shreveport, Louisiana. His first

He was a great blues and great country music fan. He and Jerry Lee were two of the most astonishing music fans I've ever met and they had total recall. You'd be amazed at all the records they listened to as kids.

—Sam Phillips

• • • •

show caught the older audience, expecting to see an old fashioned country show, by surprise. They didn't know what to think about this handsome boy who moved all over the stage. It wasn't long before the kids found out about Elvis, and a younger crowd soon dominated the audience at the Hayride shows. Elvis, with Scotty and Bill (dubbed the Blue Moon Boys), toured with the Hayride radio show through Texas, Arkansas, and Louisiana. Then it was back to Shreveport for the Saturday night shows. When not working a Hayride show, they had their own concerts.

D.J. Fontana met Elvis at the Louisiana Hayride and joined the group in 1955. He remembers those early years. "It was seven days a week, a different town every night. It got kind of old after a while. We only had one car. There'd be four guys and all the instruments. Sometimes we'd take Gene Smith or Red West with us. So it was kind of crowded. It got a bit testy sometimes with the guys cooped up in a car like that. Elvis was a super-hyper guy as a young man. He'd get through the show and would be a nervous wreck. He'd mess with the radio and talk all night, about anything as long as he was talking. One of us would walk him down the road about a mile or two. Somebody had to do it to knock the edge off him a little bit. So we'd walk down the road and they'd pick us up. We'd put him in the back seat and he'd sleep like a baby.

"We'd do a show and then go on to another city. We never read the press because we were always ahead of it. We'd leave right after the show and never knew what the press said, good or bad, whether they liked us or not. The first inkling we had it was so big was at the ole Cotton Bowl in Dallas. They rode Elvis around in this Cadillac convertible and you would have thought it was a war—the crowds and noises. I looked out there and I told Scotty, 'You know, I bet he's going to make it.' It surprised me."

In June 1955, Elvis appeared in two shows in Beaumont, Texas, to benefit the Beaumont Police Department. This may have been

A bashful Elvis at the Louisiana Hayride.

—Photo courtesy of Langston McEachern

his earliest public support of the profession that he admired so much in later years. Marty Robbins, the Maddox Brothers and Rose, Sonny James, the Bellew Twins, the Texas Stompers, and Charlene Arthur also appeared. More than twenty-four hundred tickets were sold at one dollar each.

Not all of his benefit shows were a huge success, however. On November 25, 1955, when Elvis appeared at a junior high school

—Photo courtesy of Langston McEachern.

in Port Arthur, Texas, to raise money for the city fire department, only one hundred people showed up.

While on tour Elvis did not neglect charities at home. In December 1955, he starred in a show at his alma mater, Humes High School. The show was a benefit for the school discretionary fund which helped children of poor families purchase milk. Later Elvis gave nine hundred dollars to the Humes ROTC program, which he had joined when in high school. On another occasion he paid one thousand dollars for fourteen hundred tickets to the E.H. Crump Memorial Football Game for the Blind and gave them to the student body at Humes.

Events moved fast for Elvis in the last months of 1955, after he signed a management contract with Colonel Tom Parker. Parker moved Elvis beyond the small town country and western circuit by negotiating a release from Elvis' "Louisiana Hayride" contract. Although Elvis was no longer a regular on the "Hayride," he returned on a few occasions. Two charity shows were included in his contract settlement.

Evis seemed to be glad to perform for nothing and certainly he didn't spare the gyrations.
—Pericles Alexander/Amusement Editor, The Shreveport Times

• • • •

In December 1955, and again in 1956, he performed in Shreveport to benefit the local YMCA. His last show, held at the youth building at the fairgrounds for nine thousand fans, raised over eight thousand dollars. Tickets were sold in advance for two dollars each. Pericles Alexander, of *The Shreveport Times*, described the frenzied crowd that "screamed like Zulus every time he moved a muscle."

Elvis was getting a mixed reaction on his concert tours: from teen-agers, uninhibited emotional delight; from their parents, bewilderment and disapproval. What both groups agreed on—an unspoken agreement—was that Elvis was different, somehow unique, unlike any performer they had seen before.

In 1956 Elvis achieved national fame. It was a busy year for him, full of recording sessions, television appearances, concert dates around the country, and his signing of a seven-year contract with Paramount Pictures. His first hit record on the RCA label, "Heartbreak Hotel," was released on January 27. He was seen on network television for the first time the next day. Feature stories in magazines such as *Life, Modern Screen, Look,* and *TV Guide* called Elvis America's hottest new star. And, on November 16, his first movie, "Love Me Tender," premiered. By then six of Elvis' songs had reached number one on Billboard's charts.

Still he found time for charity. On July 4, he staged a concert at Russwood Baseball Park in Memphis. The "Elvis Presley Jamboree" was a fund-raiser for *The Memphis Press-Scimitar*'s Cynthia Milk Fund and the Variety Club's Home for Convalescent Children. His hometown fans bought tickets as if it had been years since they had seen him, even though Elvis had performed in Memphis just two months earlier at the Cotton Carnival.

The 97 degree temperature that day didn't stop the fans who began gathering at 9:30 A.M. for the evening performance. The show was worth waiting for. There were over a hundred performers in the three hour, twenty minute jamboree, including four bands, five dance groups, and many singers. It was billed as "not just a rock and roll show," but it was clear the crowd was there to see Elvis. As he took the stage, the crowd suddenly came alive and rushed toward him. The City of Memphis was prepared for such a reaction. Policemen and firemen were stationed in front of the stage to maintain order. Elvis was joined by Scotty, Bill, and D.J. A special surprise was the arrival of the Jordanaires. Colonel Parker had flown them to Memphis, unannounced, to join Elvis on stage.

Elvis was particularly eager to cut loose because just a few days earlier he had been censored on "The Steve Allen Show." Before introducing Elvis, Allen had assured the audience he would provide clean, family entertainment and a new Elvis. Elvis was humiliated, forced to wear a tuxedo and sing to a hound dog. One Memphis reporter said, "Allen put Elvis in a straitjacket and still he delivered. Come out to Russwood Park and see how he can really knock a song out of the park." Fortunately, the reporter was right. Elvis

There's no denying the sheer physical power of this boy, at twenty-one he gives the impression he has lived for forty years.

—Lizabeth Scott/Co-Star
Loving You

• • • •

shouted to the crowd, "They didn't change me none," and moved his hips like he had before. His fans were thrilled. The screaming was so loud that neighboring hospitals provided increased dosages of sleeping pills to patients.

A highlight of the concert was the door prize. Elvis donated his initial ring which held fourteen diamonds. Its appraisal value was six hundred dollars, but since it belonged to Elvis, it was, of course, worth much more. Each of the seven thousand fans who attended the show desperately hoped to win the coveted prize; the winner was seventeen-year-old Roger Fakes. In addition to the ring, Elvis and Colonel Parker donated all their expenses plus five thousand souvenir booklets which were sold for the charities. Thirteen thousand dollars was raised that night.

Early in his career, Elvis made appearances for Memphis charities whenever he could. In 1957 St. Jude Children's Research Hospital was still a dream to Danny Thomas. He and the St. Jude Foundation (incorporated as ALSAC [American Lebanese Syrian Associated Charities]) had decided the hospital would be built in Memphis. A fund-raiser was staged at Russwood Park on June 28. Some of Hollywood's greatest stars, including Jane Russell, Susan Hayward, and Lou Costello, traveled to Memphis to support Danny. The highlight of the show was an unannounced appearance by Elvis. The capacity crowd screamed when Elvis came on stage. Film contracts prevented him from singing, but he thrilled the crowd with some of his famous moves. Asked to wait an hour and a half before his on-stage introduction, Elvis passed the time patiently, quietly signing autographs and posing for pictures.

Occasionally Elvis appeared on local television to support causes that he endorsed. He appeared on WMCT in Memphis to kick off the United Fund Campaign. Once again his contract prevented him from performing, but his presence drew attention to the fund-raising drive and demonstrated his support of the agency.

I was dating a sweet young lady that had a friend who had a parent that had bought a stack of tickets to that benefit. She invited me to go with a bunch of other people and they dealt out all the tickets before we went in. I just happened to end up with the right ticket. I almost fell out of my chair when they called my ticket number. It was a stroke of luck that I won Elvis' ring. I was always a fan of Elvis, always admired the guy and the way he took care of his parents and was genuinely kind to other people.

—Roger Fakes/winner of Elvis' diamond initial ring

• • • •

Imagine turning on the TV to see Elvis on "Safety Hit Parade," a public television program which aired in 1957. Though for three minutes he cautioned teen-agers to drive safely, he couldn't resist joking around. When Highway 51 (where Graceland is located) was mentioned, Elvis laughed, calling it, "The Presley Dragstrip." Perhaps Elvis was not the best spokesman for safe driving.

Elvis received a lot of attention in Memphis from his local performances and TV appearances. In 1956 the opportunity arose for him to return to his birthplace, Tupelo, Mississippi. On September 26 the entire town celebrated "Elvis Presley Day." The state's Governor, J.P. Coleman, gave Elvis a scroll and told him, "This state and the nation admire you." Mayor James Ballard gave him a guitar-shaped key to the city.

One of the things I most respected in Elvis was the fact that he never forgot that he was a man who came from good and humble people.

—Burt Reynolds

• • • •

There was a certain irony to the festivities. Eight years before, the Presleys had left Tupelo with all of their belongings packed into their car. Now, thousands of people watched a parade on Main Street, honoring the local boy who had made it to the top. Banners declared "Mississippi-Alabama Fair and Dairy Show Welcomes Tupelo's Own—In Person—Elvis Presley With His Own Show." Shop owners decorated their windows in honor of Elvis, many using the names of his hit songs. Fans had traveled from as far away as Boston to see their idol. The quiet town of Tupelo had never seen such excitement.

Elvis performed two shows at the fairgrounds stadium. The concerts were particularly significant for him. At the same fairgrounds, at the age of ten, Elvis had sung "Old Shep" and won second prize in the talent contest. Now, just eleven years later, Elvis was a phenomenal celebrity. One hundred National Guardsmen were assigned to protect him from the adoring crowd. The event earned Elvis nearly twelve thousand dollars.

That day Mayor Ballard and other Tupelo dignitaries expressed a desire for "first class park facilities which the city could not afford to give Elvis and his friends when they were growing up."

Almost a year to the day, Elvis performed again at the Mississippi-Alabama Fair in Tupelo. Twelve thousand people attended Elvis'

—Photo courtesy of Terry Wood.

show, an enormous crowd for the small town. Elvis earned twenty thousand dollars, which he immediately turned over to the mayor, and then quietly drove out of town.

The proceeds were donated to purchase his birthplace and the surrounding land for the park. The Elvis Presley Youth Foundation was formed to handle financial arrangements. Elaborate plans for the park included a large guitar-shaped swimming pool, a recreation center, baseball field, tennis courts, hiking trails to an existing lake, and many other facilities. Contractors volunteered their work to clear the fifteen-acre park.

The little shotgun house where Elvis was born still stood on the land that had once belonged to Orville Bean. Elvis and his family must have felt great satisfaction over purchasing the house because Bean had evicted them from it many years before. Who ever would have thought the Presleys would have the money to buy him out?

In these unique circumstances, Elvis not only rectified a long-festering family grievance, but he did so for the good of others: a cause that he and his childhood friends would continue to support for their entire lives.

Elvis at the Mississippi-Alabama Fair. September 26, 1956.
—Photo courtesy of Terry Wood.

• C H A P T E R • V •

THE GREATEST SHOW ON EARTH

*I*n 1958 Elvis' career was suspended by his induction into the U.S. Army. It would be two years before he would give another concert. However, recording sessions, which had been scheduled in anticipation of Elvis' departure, gave his fans new records while Elvis served in Germany. The movie "King Creole" was released during the summer of 1958 and was a huge success. Americans were proud that Elvis chose to serve as an ordinary soldier. He remained enormously popular.

On March 7, 1960, Elvis returned to Memphis after his Army discharge. By March 20 he was recording in Nashville. The new album was appropriately titled "Elvis Is Back." In May he began work on "G.I. Blues." Production of "Flaming Star" started on August 16. In October he acted in "Wild in the Country." Though Paramount Pictures had waited patiently while Elvis was in the Army, they now wanted him to fulfill his contract. He had little time for concerts.

His first Memphis show since 1957 was a benefit for hometown charities. On February 25, 1961, Elvis hosted a luncheon at the Claridge Hotel, the first event in a day devoted to raising money. Two hundred twenty-five people paid one hundred dollars each for the privilege of attending the luncheon. The Claridge's managing director confessed that, despite the price, the meal served

He doesn't want to entertain, we've asked him and he said, I'd rather not, sir.
— Major General Thomas F. Van Natta/
Commanding General
3rd Armored Division

• • • •

was the same as the restaurant menu, but the food was donated by the hotel.

Colonel Parker had paid for ninety-eight tickets to the luncheon. One of his guests was Mrs. Marie Hopper from Houston, Texas. She was one of many fans who had come to Memphis to see Elvis perform. At seventy-two years of age, Mrs. Hopper was unique. *The Memphis Press-Scimitar* reported she had been a fan for three years and was determined to see Elvis in concert. Colonel Parker read the article and arranged to meet Mrs. Hopper. He invited her to breakfast and was so impressed with her loyalty to Elvis that he invited her to be their guest at the Claridge. Mrs. Hopper immediately responded, "Oh no, I can't be up there with all those high falutin' folks." But then, realizing what she would be missing, she took the Colonel up on his offer.

A highlight of the luncheon was the presentation of awards. RCA presented Elvis with a diamond studded watch and a plaque recognizing seventy-five million record sales. He received several other awards including "Top Male Vocalist on American Bandstand" from Dick Clark.

At Ellis Auditorium, nearly ten thousand saw Elvis perform with Scotty Moore, D.J. Fontana, Boots Randolph, Floyd Cramer, and the Jordanaires. More than fifty thousand dollars from the shows was distributed among thirty-eight charities. Ten percent went to the Elvis Presley Youth Center in Tupelo. Twenty-four hundred dollars was given to a fund designated for a memorial to Memphians killed in World War II and the Korean War.

Elvis' next concert was also a tribute to America's war dead. On March 25 Elvis appeared in Honolulu, Hawaii. Some months earlier, newspapers had run a story on the Pacific War Memorial Commission's efforts to build a memorial to the USS Arizona. During the attack on Pearl Harbor on December 7, 1941, the ship

OPPOSITE:
—Photo courtesy of Linda Everett.

Ellis Auditorium, Memphis
February 25, 1961.
—Photo courtesy of Bill Burk.

was sunk with more than one thousand crew members aboard. The Memorial Commission had worked for sixteen years to raise the money needed to honor this tragic loss of life. In 1960 they were halfway to their goal. Another quarter of a million dollars was needed but donations had ceased.

In a desperate attempt to rejuvenate fund-raising, the War Memorial Commission appealed to *The Honolulu Advertiser.* George Chaplin, editor of the newpaper, wrote to fifteen hundred mainland papers asking them to run editorials on December 7, 1960. His letter read in part, "the men's remains are still entombed in a rusted mess of junk, a disgrace to the nation." It ended with an appeal for contributions.

The response was less than overwhelming: a few thousand dollars were added to the trust fund. Colonel Parker read the editorial in a Los Angeles newpaper. He called Chaplin and told him Elvis was scheduled to begin work on the film "Blue Hawaii" in March. Then he offered to donate an Elvis Presley concert if all of the proceeds went to the project.

A crowd of three thousand was at the Honolulu airport to greet Elvis. As the plane touched down, screams of "Elvis" filled the air. Honolulu and military police barely controlled the fans behind a wire fence. Other celebrities, including Minnie Pearl and Jimmy Stewart, stepped off the plane with Elvis, but no one seemed to notice them.

People lined the streets as the entourage traveled from the airport. At the Hawaiian Village Hotel the police weren't prepared for the mayhem that followed. Hundreds of women broke the police barrier, trying to get close to Elvis. Minnie Pearl recalls that she had never before seen anything like it and was frightened. Naïvely, Elvis didn't think his fans would ever hurt him. And they wouldn't, intentionally. Still, the danger was very real; the excited

I began to get these chilling feelings that maybe I didn't want to be all that close to Elvis. I was afraid I'd be trampled by that mob of screaming women.

—Minnie Pearl

• • • •

—Photo courtesy of the
Honolulu Star-Bulletin

—Photo courtesy of Linda Everett

Elvis held a press conference for students of a Hawaiian high school. March 1961.
—Photo courtesy of the *Honolulu Star-Bulletin*

crowd would have done anything to touch Elvis or take home a souvenir of his clothing.

The concert was scheduled for 8:30 that evening at Bloch Arena in the Pearl Harbor Navy Base. Ticket prices ranged from three to one hundred dollars. Elvis and Colonel Parker donated the concert; but as if that wasn't enough, they bought their own tickets—hundred dollar ringside seats. When a high-ranking military officer asked Parker for complimentary passes, he was told that Elvis' own father had to pay for his admission. No free passes were given to anyone who could afford to support the cause. Nevertheless, Parker and Elvis bought ringside seats for patients from Honolulu Tripler Army Hospital.

Souvenir sales from the concert (photographs of Elvis which sold for fifty cents each) were donated to another charity, the Pearl Harbor Youth Foundation.

Elvis opened his show with "Heartbreak Hotel." The crowd screamed so loudly he could hardly be heard. For the last time he wore the gold lamé suit coat which his fans recognized from the cover of his 1959 album, "50,000 Elvis Fans Can't Be Wrong–Elvis Gold Records, Volume 2."

His show earned sixty-two thousand dollars for the War Memorial Commission. No less important was the publicity the event received. Elvis created new interest in the project, stimulating donations from around the country. On Memorial Day 1962, just fourteen months after Elvis' benefit concert, the Memorial to the USS Arizona was dedicated. At the opening ceremonies, a large proclamation, recognizing all who contributed, including Elvis, was displayed in the Bell Room of the Memorial.

The United States Navy was appreciative of Elvis' efforts. Before Elvis was introduced at the concert, a telegram from the Secretary of the Navy was read. Earlier that day, Navy Commander Herbert Gimple presented Elvis with a plaque. Elvis was made an honorary member of the Pacific War Memorial Commission and was given a certificate signed by Admiral Nimitz.

On Sunday afternoon, after the concert, we were down on Waikiki Beach. We were having a big time down there and said we wished Elvis could come down and be with us, and we turned and looked up at his penthouse which was facing the ocean. And he was standing on the balcony of that penthouse, alone, looking down at us. He was just standing there, a solitary figure, lonely-looking, looking down at us having such a good time. He literally was a prisoner because of his fans. He couldn't come down. He couldn't go anywhere.

—Minnie Pearl

• • • •

NEXT THREE PHOTOS
—Courtesy of *The Honolulu Advertiser.*

It's wonderful to get a chance in your lifetime to do something of this nature. In contrast to entertaining, an opportunity such as this is especially satisfying.

—Elvis, discussing his benefit concert for the USS Arizona

• • • •

Years later, upon hearing of Elvis' death, Rear Admiral R.S. Wentworth Jr., commandant of the 14th Naval district, sent a telegram to Vernon Presley: "Elvis Presley was greatly admired by the Navy men and women, past and present, of the 50th State. Your great loss is deeply shared by all of us who remember Elvis Presley as an outstanding American who loved his country and felt a kindred spirit with American men and women in uniform." On August 17, 1977, the U.S. Navy laid a wreath at the Memorial in Elvis' honor.

Of all of Elvis' accomplishments, his contribution to the USS Arizona Memorial is the one he was most proud of. When Elvis and Colonel Parker visited the Memorial on August 15, 1965, Elvis placed two, five-foot high wreaths there. One arrangement held 1,177 carnations, symbolizing the number of men lost with the Arizona. In 1968 he and Priscilla returned without, he thought, advance notice. But to his dismay the media were there. Elvis considered this visit a private matter—not a publicity stunt. He preferred that only a select few Navy men should know of his visits. He never again visited the USS Arizona although he intended to. In March 1977, while vacationing in Hawaii, his plans were canceled when Vernon suffered a mild heart attack in Memphis.

Elvis' contribution was recognized at the USS Arizona Memorial until 1980 when the National Park Service assumed control of the Memorial from the U.S. Navy. Claiming that the proclamation which listed him as a contributor wasn't adequately protected from the salt air, the Park Service removed it. For many years, there was nothing at the Memorial to tell visitors of Elvis' involvement. But through the diligence of Elvis' fans, a copy of the proclamation has recently been put on display in the visitors center.

The show for the USS Arizona Memorial was his last live show for seven years. He rejuvenated his performing career with his

PHOTO ON PAGE 61:
—Courtesy of Graceland.

Elvis and Colonel Parker at
the USS Arizona Memorial.
—Photo courtesy of Graceland.

NBC Singer Special (now called the '68 Comeback), a televised concert performed before a studio audience. D.J. Fontana recalls Elvis' extreme nervousness before the show. He was afraid people wouldn't like him. D.J. told him, "Go out there and kill'em like you always do. You always have. They'll get on your side again." And they did.

In 1969 he returned to the stage at the International Hotel in Las Vegas. Elvis joked about his celebrity status in the two-page ad for the opening. Large, bold letters declared "Sammy Shore, The Imperials, The Sweet Inspirations, Musical Conductor — Bobby Morris." A listing of Elvis' musicians followed. In much smaller print at the bottom of the ad was the statement, "P.S. I'm in the show too! . . . Elvis."

Elvis did not limit himself to a rock and roll nostalgia act, a quick rendition of his hit songs. He created a show worthy of Las Vegas show business. He rehearsed everything: the timing of the lights, the orchestra accompaniment, the harmonies of his vocalists. His show was spectacular. Before the start of each performance, just before the first notes of the theme for "2001 — A Space Odyssey" were heard, the air tingled with excitement. The audience could somehow sense when Elvis arrived backstage. One could feel their anticipation. He dressed in extravagant theatrical jumpsuits and sang for nearly two hours, blending rock energy and ballads. While singing his love songs, he walked to his female fans. They rushed to him for a scarf, a touch, or a kiss. Elvis loved spontaneity and the give-and-take between an artist and the audience. He closed his performances with a flourish, and left the stage exhausted.

We talked about the early days and the recent days. We talked about the people we admired — each other — and people who tried to really perform from the heart, with soul, as opposed to trying to make commercial records.

—Roy Orbison.

• • • •

One reporter said, "Elvis has become **E L V I S**." Every aspect of his shows—his jumpsuits, the scarves he gave away, his movements—became part of the Elvis legend. His friend, Janelle, remembers he was magic.

How can I explain the Elvis charisma? It became an evening of undisputed talent, interpersed with moments of both rare wit and nostalgia. When he sang "Unchained Melody," one could close their eyes and envision themselves being tapped by his magic wand and transported to a world that few are privileged to enjoy.

From the stage the Elvis charisma spread like a fog, and both young and old succumbed to its magic. The very old in the audience would relive their memories, the middle-aged waged an inner war with their frustrations, and the young well knew that wishing could perhaps make it so, and they too began to dream of the impossible.

At the International Hotel (later named the Las Vegas Hilton) Elvis was booked for one month engagements. He played to larger crowds than any other performer. When he performed at the Sahara Tahoe in Lake Tahoe, Nevada, the crowds were as great. Elvis never again stopped touring. He traveled the country playing over a thousand shows; almost all were sell-out crowds, and he was doing what he loved best.

Though the concerts were a lucrative business, they also provided Elvis with a unique opportunity to raise funds for charity. On February 23, 1973, Elvis closed at the Hilton Hotel after performing in fifty-one shows. The month-long engagement had brought in twenty-seven thousand dollars in souvenir sales. Elvis and Colonel Parker donated the entire sum to the Southern Nevada Society for the Aurally Handicapped. In January 1974, Elvis returned for a two week commitment. This time the Sisters of the Home of the Good Shepherd received the money from the souvenir booth. In March 1975, thirteen thousand dollars raised by the souvenir stand went to a fund to aid Adoption of Special Kids. In

I got tired of singing to the guys I beat up in the motion pictures.
—Elvis

• • • •

1976 seventeen thousand dollars was donated to the American Heart Association. Because not all contributions were publicized, few people know the full extent of the donations earned through the Las Vegas shows. The amount is believed to be greater than three hundred thousand dollars.

Elvis adopted the same policy for other concerts. On two different occasions, in Lake Tahoe, souvenir sales were donated to the Barton Memorial Hospital Auxiliary's efforts to build a coronary care unit. Elvis followed this contribution with a rare Nevada benefit concert at Del Webb's Sahara Tahoe, at 3:00 A.M. on Mothers' Day, 1973. Elvis loved the night life, but so do the people in this land of all-night casinos, and a large crowd turned out to see his show. The concert was a gift to his mother, Gladys, in whose memory he performed to support the hospital. A plaque, which hangs in the lobby, reads, "In memory of Mrs. Gladys Presley through the financial support of her son Elvis."

Late in 1972, Elvis Presley announced plans for a concert production broadcast to the world by satellite television, an idea which appealed to his sense of the dramatic. It was unprecedented showmanship, a concert viewed around the world by the one entertainer whose name was recognizable everywhere.

Perhaps only a phenomenon like Elvis Presley could pull off such a coup, at such a wicked showgoing time—12:30 A.M. curtain—yet draw a full house.

—Wayne Harada/Reporter
The *Honolulu Advertiser.*

•   •   •   •

It has been said Elvis agreed to the show rather than give in to the constant demands for world tours. Elvis, of course, never toured beyond the North American continent. The show was arranged particularly for the growing Asian television markets. Elvis was to perform at the Honolulu International Center, in Hawaii on January 14, at 12:30 A.M., an hour that would broadcast in prime time in Asia. European television viewers would receive the show the next day. Americans, who could see Elvis perform in many cities, would not watch the show until a later date.

The technical problems of this broadcast made it the most expensive television event of the time, costing $2.5 million. Colonel Parker insured a profit from the fees demanded of televison networks and advertisers. Parker even negotiated with United Airlines, who supplied travelogs for the television special. At the same time RCA announced that a recording of the concert was to be released simultaneously throughout the world, a first in the recording industry. Appropriately, the album cover portrayed the planet Earth and a satellite in orbit, and was called, "Aloha From Hawaii Via Satellite."

While in Hawaii on his November 1972 tour Elvis announced that ticket sales for the "Aloha From Hawaii" show would be donated to the Kui Lee Cancer Fund. The charity was named for Kuiokalani Lee who had written "I'll Remember You," a song Elvis had recorded in 1966 for the movie "Paradise Hawaiian Style," and had sung in his Hawaiian shows. Kui Lee died of cancer shortly after Elvis' recording was released.

Tickets were sold for the dress rehearsal show on January 12, and for the January 14 concert, but the method of sale was somewhat unconventional. There were no admission fees. All that was required to obtain a ticket was a donation to the Cancer Fund. Any amount, no matter how small, was acceptable. The public responded generously. The city of Honolulu was grateful that Elvis was again donating his effort and talent to Hawaiian causes. Mayor Frank F. Fasi declared January 13 "Elvis Presley Day" in Honolulu.

The television special began with a picture of the satellite, and the sound of a transmission signal. Then the name "Elvis" appeared in several foreign languages, each language flashing in time with the signal beep. Elvis strode on stage wearing a white jumpsuit emblazoned with an American eagle. He had asked his costume designer, Bill Belew, for a design which would emphasize his patriotism.

The jumpsuit was originally crafted with a calf-length cape. This was too heavy and Belew made a shorter version which Elvis wore on stage. Today, the original cape, which Elvis did not wear, is on display at Graceland.

The crowd's reaction to Elvis' presence was wild and enthusiastic. Elvis was at his peak. As he took the microphone, the audience was under his full control. Caught up in the excitement of the moment, they cheered every song. Elvis paced his show, and gave them what they wanted. During the romantic ballads, he accepted leis and kisses from his female admirers. Sometimes he handed a scarf or handkerchief to an overwhelmed fan. For the song, "Steamroller Blues," he put a sexy edge in his voice. Elvis had them screaming in delight with a turn of his face, a knowing look in his eyes. He finished every song powerfully, most with a karate pose. His band, all veterans of his Las Vegas show, seemed to know his every move.

Near the end of the show Elvis announced that the concert had raised seventy-five thousand dollars for the Kui Lee Cancer Fund. This was triple the expected amount. Two girls in particular wanted to thank Elvis for his donation. Kui Lee's daughters stood near the stage hoping that Elvis would notice them so they could give him a lei, but they couldn't find the opportunity. Elvis probably never knew they were there.

I didn't have to move out of my seat to get it.

—Bruce Spinks/the man who caught Elvis' cape.

• • • •

For the last song, Elvis sang "Can't Help Falling In Love," a hit from his "Blue Hawaii" film. Charlie Hodge placed the white cape, which Elvis was to have worn during the entire show, on his neck. While the back-up singers carried the song, he strolled for the last time to the fans. One member of the audience gave him a golden crown. At the song's finale he threw the cape into the crowd, and strolled off the stage.

This event was broadcast live to more than a billion people in nearly forty countries. Elvis had captured 91.8 percent of the viewing

audience in the Philippines and 70 percent in Hong Kong. Each country reported unprecedented ratings. Even some citizens of Communist China, who had access to Hong Kong and Macao television, watched the show.

Elvis had achieved something remarkable—a performance that would be remembered worldwide for years to come. His televised image from this show was so influential that more impersonators copy the jumpsuit and perform the songs from that concert than from any other period of his life. He entertained "half the world" with one performance. "Bringing the world closer together," may sound like a cliché, but in this case it was true. Elvis, in "Aloha From Hawaii," gave people of different nations and cultures a shared, joyous experience. They would talk about that moment for years to come. Not only was he still the King of Rock and Roll, he was an ambassador of good will.

Elvis continued his role as ambassador when he heard of a disaster in his home state. In January 1975, a tornado struck the southwest region of Mississippi. Seven people were killed and more than a hundred were injured. Property damage was extensive. Elvis reacted to news of the disaster by immediately making plans for a concert. In a telegram sent to Colonel Parker, Elvis said, "I want to help all I can for the state I was born in."

Elvis may have had recollections of a tornado that devastated his hometown when he was just one year old. On April 5, 1936, Tupelo was hit by one of the worst storms in history. The Presleys were not injured but the tornado damaged nearly everything around their home. More than two hundred people were killed and more than a thousand were injured. At least nine hundred homes were destroyed. Makeshift hospitals were set up all over town.

Today, at Priceville Cemetery, the effect of the horror can still be seen. One plot holds the graves and markers of eleven children

His recorded voice has been heard by more people in the world than that of any other performing artist in the history of the recording industry. His singing has touched each of us and been a part of many people.

—RCA employee newsletter

•   •   •   •

PRECEDING PHOTOGRAPH
The "Aloha From Hawaii"
Concert.

—Photo courtesy
of Graceland.

and their parents, an entire family killed by the storm, buried on a hill overlooking a small valley of unmarked graves.

This concert was to be Elvis' first show in Mississippi since his Tupelo benefit in 1957. Colonel Parker later refused to contract shows in the state because of the state's exorbitant entertainment tax. When Hurricane Camille damaged the Mississippi Gulf Coast in 1969, Elvis was asked to give a benefit show for the victims. He declined and sent a cash donation instead. Elvis' fans lobbied successfully for a reduction in the tax and, in 1974, Jackson businessmen began asking Colonel Parker to schedule a show in the city's new coliseum.

Elvis' decision to perform for the tornado victims of 1975 made headline news. The Governor's press secretary responded in one interview, "Only God and Colonel Parker know when this concert is going to take place, and Parker hasn't told God when yet." The release of the date and location of the concert was publicized within less than a week.

The long-awaited concert was scheduled for May 5 at the ten thousand seat Mississippi Coliseum in Jackson. Tickets sold out within hours. Mississippi Governor Bill Waller bought two hundred tickets: ten for his family and friends, the remainder for legislators and other associates. The Governor created a controversy; some people felt the ticket distribution was unfair. But one person who didn't complain was Colonel Parker. Tickets were in such great demand that he quickly added three commercial concerts in Jackson to Elvis' tour schedule.

The benefit concert raised over one hundred thousand dollars for a special fund to assist tornado victims. Elvis, once again, had bought his own ticket, in addition to handling all other costs. McComb Mayor, Johnny Thompson, presented Elvis with a certificate of appreciation.

This concert marked the last time Elvis appeared in concert for the sole purpose of raising money for a particular cause. But his concerts were only one means that Elvis used to assist those in need.

—Photo courtesy of Linda Everett.

Elvis with Mississippi Governor,
Bill Waller.
May 5, 1975.
—Photo courtesy of Elizabeth Hill.

· C H A P T E R · VI ·

THE SEASON OF GIVING

Christmas was always a special holiday to the Presley family. When Elvis was a boy, the family had little money but celebrated the day in as big a fashion as they could afford. Even in the toughest times, Elvis always had a big Christmas, surrounded by family and friends.

As Elvis' income grew, so did the celebration. Almost every year Elvis hosted Christmas at Graceland. The house and grounds were decorated early in the month in enthusiastic anticipation. Blue lights lined the long drive to the mansion. More lights were strung on the roofline of the house. Lighted Christmas trees, each a vivid color, adorned the front of the home. In the early sixties Elvis commissioned a life-size Nativity scene for the lawn. Sculpted figures were placed in a thirty-foot tall stable and flood lights made the scene more dramatic at night. The display was so spectacular that Elvis liked to park his car across the street and admire it. Though the scene was the same year after year, residents of Memphis never tired of it and often drove by to look at it.

Elvis delighted in Christmas shopping and playing Santa Claus. Goldsmith's Department Store in Memphis opened after hours to allow Elvis to shop in privacy without being surrounded by a crowd. Though Elvis enjoyed giving presents, he also liked receiving them, ripping off the carefully wrapped paper to see what was inside. Friends and family had trouble buying a gift for someone who could buy anything he wanted, but even if Elvis already had one or several of the items given him, he acted as if he had always wanted this one. He was always pleased by his cousin, Harold Loyd's, present, even though Harold gave him the same thing every Christmas: a candy bar, as a reminder of their childhood poverty.

In a lot of ways Christmas at Graceland was very traditional. Friends and family filled the house with laughter. Gifts were exchanged and everyone gathered around the table for a holiday meal. And Elvis always inspired a certain playfulness. Christmas night usually brought everyone outside to the estate grounds. Elvis' annual fireworks show was rivaled only by the city of Memphis' Fourth of July celebration. Elvis spent more than a thousand dollars each Christmas to provide an elaborate display for his family and friends.

But the Christmas season can be one of sadness for those who do not fare as well. George Klein remembers one holiday when Elvis received a letter from the widow of Dewey Phillips. Phillips, the disc jockey who was the first to play an Elvis record in 1954, had died penniless. Mrs. Phillips wrote that she had little for her young boys. Elvis sent her a check for one thousand dollars. Another Christmas night, Elvis decided to visit the city jail. "It's the only place open now," he explained to his confused friends. The prisoners and guards made quite a fuss when Elvis and his party walked through the jail. George and Elvis spotted someone they knew behind bars, a former classmate from Humes. "Elvis! Get me out of here," the man shouted. Elvis paid his bail, and the jailers set him free.

As much as he enjoyed the festivities of the season, Elvis never forgot the true meaning of Christmas. He spread holiday cheer beyond the gates of Graceland. Each year, in the true Christmas spirit, he donated money to many charities.

He was such a good person that he just wanted to alleviate everybody's problems.

—Marty Lacker

• • • •

—Photo courtesy of Linda Everett

Elvis began this practice early in his career. In December 1957, he drove up to make a contribution to the Mile-O-Dimes booth on Main Street. Elvis pulled out one thousand dollars in bills of all denominations. *The Commercial Appeal* reported, "It was a typically big-hearted Presley gesture and the crowd that gathered there loved it." Elvis stayed at the booth only a few minutes, then sped away with a police escort. His contribution to the Christmas Fund was more than the money he gave. His appearance inspired many others to give to the charity.

He felt the good Lord blessed him when he gave to others. For this reason he gave so impulsively. He always felt his talent was given to him as a gift from our Lord. He felt he should share that gift with others, whether through his voice or through monetary means. He gave for the joy and self-satisfaction that stemmed from giving.

—Ed Parker

• • • •

Elvis' fans loved to give him gifts. After Elvis sang "Teddy Bear" in the movie "Loving You," he received hundreds of teddy bears from his fans. In December 1957, he donated the stuffed animals to the National Foundation for Infantile Paralysis.

The teddy bears were auctioned to raise money for the March of Dimes. He received a special thank you from the 1955 poster girl, eight-year-old Mary Kosloski, who stopped by Graceland to give Elvis a big hug and a kiss.

While in the Army, Elvis continued to play Santa Claus. In 1959 he mailed a check for one thousand dollars to the Memphis Mile-O-Dimes Christmas Basket Fund. That same year he donated money to the Steinmuehie Orphanage near Friedberg, Germany. One hundred and fifteen children received Christmas gifts and had a Christmas party. Elvis also arranged for many of the children to spend the holidays with Army families.

In 1961 Elvis performed in Memphis to raise money for local organizations. The following year his film and recording obligations kept him too busy for a repeat performance. Instead, he drafted checks to those charities that had benefited the previous year, and added several new ones to the list. In 1962 he donated fifty thousand dollars to fifty associations. Elvis continued these annual donations faithfully until his death.

—Photo courtesy of
AP Wide World Photos.

In the early years Elvis distributed his contributions himself. In December 1963, representatives of fifty-eight organizations assembled at the mayor's office at city hall. Even the recipients couldn't resist asking for his autograph and he signed the envelopes that contained the checks. That year the organizations had something special for him, a six-foot tall plaque. Elvis joked, "Good grief. That's beautiful, but I may have to build a room just to keep it in." Eventually, he did. Today, that plaque is in the trophy room at Graceland. Inscribed on it are the names of fifty organizations that Elvis supported.

Any appearance by Elvis in public brought out his fans and the media. Eventually he stopped making personal presentations. He either mailed the contributions or asked his father to deliver them. One newspaper in 1968 reported Elvis had driven his black Lincoln limousine to the Whitehaven post office and dropped one hundred and forty envelopes, addressed to charities, into the mail.

The yearly event made news, but Elvis felt giving was a personal matter. He asked that the amount of money not be publicly disclosed. Newspapers always reported the story and listed the organizations Elvis supported. When amounts of money weren't available, they reported the sum in the thousands. Sometimes they reported amounts given in previous years. In 1968 they disclosed donations of one hundred and five thousand dollars given in 1966. Not all of the organizations were in Memphis. Many were Nevada charities that Elvis had become acquainted with during his Las Vegas shows. Some were in California. Others were in Arizona, Nebraska, and South Dakota. One can only guess how Elvis became involved with them.

Elvis approached his annual gifts with the spontaneity that he shared with his family and friends. He considered each charity and gave what he wanted to. Just as one might not spend the

I don't think that Elvis let anybody down. Personally, I don't think he owed anything to anybody. I think that, as it was, he did more for most people than they'll ever have done for them in their lives.

—Bruce Springsteen

• • • •

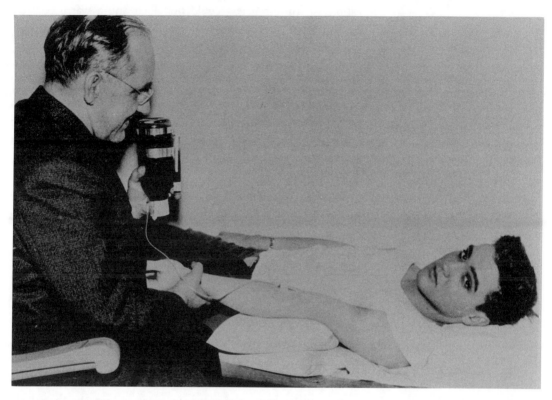

Elvis donating blood in Germany.
—Photo courtesy of Linda Everett.

same amount of money on every Christmas gift purchased, Elvis varied the amounts of the donations. The list was modified every year. Many beneficiaries received something from Elvis annually. Some were omitted; others were added.

Elvis did not have a favorite charity. He gave to any that caught his attention. Almost as if trying to cover all of the bases for a better world, Elvis helped nearly every type of organization. He supported medical research so that we might have a world free of cancer, cerebral palsy, muscular dystrophy, and other debilitating diseases. He gave to the Salvation Army and other similar organizations so the homeless could find food and a warm bed. He supported the Elk's Club, the Junior League, and numerous other service-oriented associations.

Elvis had a soft spot in his heart for children. Donations were made to many children's homes and hospitals in an attempt to end childhood suffering. Day care centers in impoverished neighborhoods received Elvis' support so that parents might work for a better home for their children. He supported boys clubs, girls clubs, and YMCAs to bring recreation to those that might have only the streets as a playground.

Elvis was the epitome of the Biblical joy of giving. He gave without wanting anything in return. He loved to make people happy.
—Marty Lacker

• • • •

Elvis recognized no boundaries of race or religion. As a boy, he listened to and admired black blues and gospel musicians. In those days of segregation and Southern repression of blacks, Elvis remained untouched by the prejudice that existed around him. He took each individual as he found him. Lauderdale Courts, Elvis' home while in high school, was located near the Pinch District, a predominantly Jewish neighborhood. Elvis frequently visited the Jewish Neighborhood House, and even took singing lessons there.

Many of the organizations that Elvis supported had black or Jewish associations. He gave to the Orange Mound Day Nursery for Negroes (as it was called then), the Jesse Mahan Day Care Center for Negro children in the Dixie Homes Area, the Abe Scharff Branch of the YMCA for Negroes, the Jewish Community Center, and Memphis Hebrew Academy. And he gave to nearly every denomination, to Baptist, Catholic, and Episcopal organizations.

Today it is difficult to determine the amount of money Elvis gave each December. The organizations have kept incomplete records and what information they have is filed away in attics and closets. It's doubtful that a complete listing of beneficiaries could be obtained. But Elvis never intended the amount of donations or the total number of recipients to become public information.

His reasons for giving were greater than a play for publicity or a desire to be known as a nice guy.

His donations were not even claimed as income tax deductions. Elvis explained, "The joy is in the giving. I don't want the money back." He gave from the heart. When he sang, "If I Can Dream," he wished for a world free of pain and suffering. Elvis did more than daydream; he acted. That year he said, "I am happy that I am in the position to help the organizations in a small way. I believe in the charities and what they do for many people. We should all do more to assist."

I could never become so rich that I would forget what it's like to be poor.

—Elvis

• • • •

CHRISTMAS DONATIONS
1957-1977

Abe Scharff YMCA
Alpine Guild
Arthritis Foundation
Ave Maria Guild Home for the Aged
Baptist Children's Home
Beale Street Elk's Club
Bethany Home
Boys Club of Palm Springs
Boys Club of Phoenix, Arizona
Boys Town of Memphis
Braille Institute of America
Camp Courage
Commercial Appeal Fresh Air Fund
Convent of the Good Shepherd
Crippled Children's Hospital
Cynthia Milk Fund
Duration Club, Inc.
Elk's Blues Bowl Committee
Elvis Presley Youth Center of Tupelo
Episcopal Home for Girls
Exchange Club
Family Service of Memphis
Father Flanagan's Boys Town of Nebraska
Foundation for the Junior Blind
Fraternal Order of Police
Girls Club of Memphis
Goodwill Home for Children
Goodwill Industries
Happy Acres
Home for Incurables
Hospital for Crippled Adults
Howard Manor Christian Home
Jesse Mahan Center
Jewish Community Center
John Tracy Clinic
Junior League
Kennedy Hospital Christmas Fund
Kidney Foundation
King's Daughter's Trinity Circle

Le Bonheur Children's Hospital
Le Bonheur Club
Les Passes
Lions Club
Little City of the Mid-South
Los Angeles County Heart Association
Mary Galloway Home
Memphis Epilepsy Foundation
Memphis Heart Association
Memphis Hebrew Academy
Memphis Mother's Service
Memphis-Press Scimitar Good Fellows
Memphis-Shelby County Council for Retarded Children
Memphis Speech and Hearing Center
Memphis Union Mission
Mid-South Cancer Research
Mile-0-Dimes
Mother's YMCA Canteen
Muscular Dystrophy
Neighborhood House
Oncological Research Foundation
Orange Mound Day Nursery
Palm Springs Jaycees
Porter-Leath Children's Home
Salvation Army
Sarah Brown YMCA
Shelby United Neighbors
Sheltered Workshop
St. Gerard Hall
St. Joseph Indian School of Chamberlain, South Dakota
St. Jude Children's Research Hospital
St. Peter's Orphanage
The Thalians of Beverly Hills, California
United Cerebral Palsy
United Fund of the Desert Communities
Variety Club of Memphis
West Tennessee Cancer Clinic
Whitehaven Jaycees
Youth Service

OPPOSITE:
—Photo courtesy of Linda Everett.

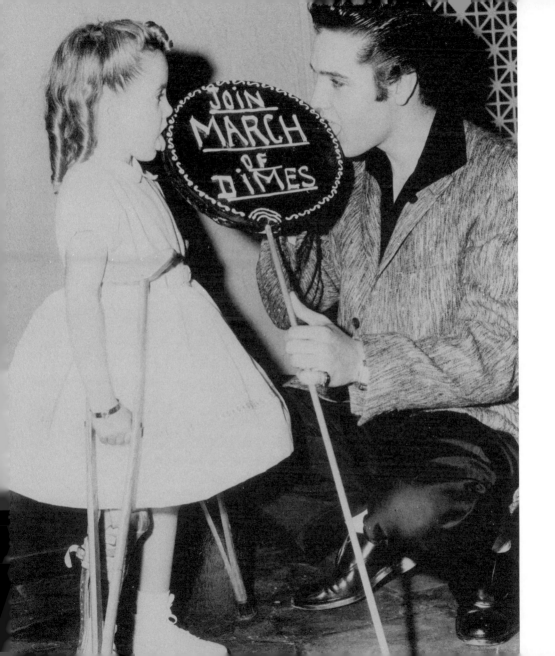

IF I CAN DREAM

There must be lights burning brighter somewhere
Got to be birds flying higher, in a sky more blue
If I can dream of a better land,
Where all my brothers walk hand in hand
Tell me why, oh why can't my dreams come true.

There must be peace and understanding sometime
Strong winds of promise will blow away doubt and fear
If I can dream of a warmer sun
Where hope keeps shining on everyone
Tell me why, oh why won't that sun appear.

We're lost in a cloud with too much rain
We're trapped in a world with too much pain
But as long as a man has the strength to dream
He can redeem his soul and fly.

Deep in my heart there's a trembling question
Still I am sure that the answer's going to come somehow
Out there in the dark there's a beckoning candle
And while I can think, while I can walk,
While I can stand, while I can walk
While I can dream, *may* my dreams come true right now
Let it come true right now.

W. Earl Brown. 1968. Gladys Music, Warner/Chappel Music. ASCAP.

Those Who Knew Him

Gary Pepper and family
in Hollywood.
—Photo courtesy of Will McDaniel.

HASN'T THE LORD BLESSED US, MOTHER?

*I*n one of his rare interviews, Elvis declared, "I know what poverty is. I lived it for a long time. But my mama and daddy kept struggling. They did everything possible for me." As a child he dreamed of making their lives easier. He watched them work at tiring, menial jobs. In Tupelo, Vernon accepted whatever jobs he could find and sometimes had to travel to find employment. Gladys worked at a number of jobs to supplement Vernon's meager salary. At times she took in laundry or worked as a sewing machine operator, a waitress, or a nurse's aide. Then she took care of the men in her family, cleaning and boosting their spirits. Still, the family never had enough money to cover their bills. The rent often caught up with them, and they were forced to move to yet another dingy apartment or rental house.

In 1948 Vernon sought work in Memphis. Elvis recalled, "We were broke, man, broke. I remember we left Tupelo overnight. Dad packed all our belongings in boxes and put them on the top and in the trunk of a 1939 Plymouth. We just headed to Memphis. Things had to be better."

The Presley family—Vernon, Gladys, Elvis, and Vernon's mother, Minnie Mae—moved into a one room apartment on Poplar Avenue.

Vernon found work with the United Paint Company. It was a steady job, something he had not found in Tupelo. Within a year the family moved into Lauderdale Courts, a federally-funded housing project. It was not luxurious, but at least it had two bedrooms.

In many ways, life for the Presleys improved in Memphis. Still they struggled to get ahead. Vernon's job was painfully boring, nothing more than stacking paint cans day after day. His back often bothered him, and the fear of losing the ability to lift haunted him. Gladys continued to work. She worried about the inspections of the apartment by the housing authority and sometimes stayed up all night cleaning in preparation.

No matter how tired or frustrating their days were, his parents rarely complained. Gladys and Vernon tried to convince Elvis they weren't poor and struggled to give him things he wanted. They wouldn't allow him to work when they felt it jeopardized his studies. But Elvis saw through their well-intended deceptions. He learned from them to face adversity head-on and to trust in the Lord. It was the Presleys' faith, and their love for each other, that sustained them.

The one thing I bought as a star that meant the most to me was a fifty dollar picture of Jesus I gave to my parents.

—Elvis

• • • •

Elvis never forgot the sacrifices Gladys and Vernon made for him. When he began performing, much of his income went to his parents. During the tours at the beginning of his career he wired money home to assist with the bills. He purchased things to make their work easier. For Gladys, he bought two hand-held mixers, one for each end of the kitchen so she wouldn't have to walk very far when she needed one.

In May 1956, Elvis bought his parents their first home. The forty thousand dollar ranch-style house at 1034 Audubon Drive was in a fashionable neighborhood. But doctors, lawyers, and other professional people who lived there were not impressed with the new residents. They thought the Presleys were nice enough, but a class difference separated them. The people in this neighborhood didn't hang their laundry out to dry as Gladys did. The Presleys were simple people who, in spite of Elvis' success, didn't put on airs. Many of their old friends from Lauderdale Courts visited them. The neighbors never quite accepted the working people who drove up to the Presley home in old cars, wearing greasy work clothes.

Their children, however, were thrilled. The most famous young man in the world lived in the neighborhood. He would ride around in one of his cars, or on a motorcycle. Sometimes he would play football with his friends in nearby Audubon Park. The girls scribbled love notes on the Presley mailbox and hoped he would pick them for his next ride on the motorcycle. It was cool to cruise past 1034 Audubon Drive. At nearly all hours the neighborhood was filled with teen-agers driving by or parked in front of the Presley home. The next-door neighbor complained when his lawn died from the number of kids trampling on it.

The neighbors finally asked Elvis and his family to move. At first he refused and offered to buy their houses. He probably had more money than all of them put together. But that wasn't what the neighbors wanted to hear and they declined Elvis' offer.

Problems with the neighbors didn't dampen Elvis' enthusiasm; he was so pleased to provide a home for his family. And there were other things he wanted them to have. In September he gave his mother his pink Cadillac. She didn't drive, but that seemed a minor point to Elvis. Gladys enjoyed riding in the car. The Presleys used it for leisurely Sunday outings. Elvis bought many other cars and gave most of them away, but he never parted with his mother's pink Cadillac.

It was while riding in the pink Cadillac that Elvis' parents discovered Graceland. They noticed a house for sale on U.S. Highway

It happened very fast, to all of us. To my mother, my father, and all of us, you know, everything happened overnight, and so we had to adjust to a lot of things very quickly. A lot of good things, I might add.

—Elvis

• • • •

Elvis with his proud parents at the Tupelo Fair.
—Photo courtesy of Terry Wood.

51 South in the Whitehaven community. It was a Southern Colonial with eighteen rooms, nestled on fourteen acres. It was named after the great-aunt of the owner's wife. Elvis' parents loved it.

Elvis was away at the time and Vernon called him to tell him about the house. Elvis didn't need to see it; if his parents liked it, that was enough. He told Vernon to buy it. Elvis liked the name

Graceland and never changed it. When Gladys' son was born in the two-room shotgun house in Tupelo, she couldn't have imagined he would one day have a mansion for her to live in. But Elvis never wanted anything less than a mansion for her.

Sadly, Elvis lost his mother the year after they moved into Graceland. Her health had never been robust. The more successful Elvis became, the more she worried about him. He was pulled away from her and she couldn't protect him. Critics made fun of him and girls rushed at him. Furthermore, she didn't feel she could live up to the role of "Elvis Presley's Mother." She wasn't comfortable giving interviews or being photographed. She worried about not being pretty enough and dieted to lose weight. Elvis' career had moved so quickly she had little time to adjust. Her health declined. In March 1958, Elvis was inducted into the Army. Now her only son was to face life-threatening dangers far from her. It was too much for her to bear. She died in August, just one month before his transfer to Germany.

Elvis was devastated. He lamented, "It wasn't only losing a mother, it was like losing a friend, a companion, someone to talk to." Gladys had been the person closest to him. He relied on her strength and wisdom. Though he had many other women in his life, he never again found the security he had felt with Gladys. His successes were somehow incomplete without her to share them with. Many people who were with Elvis during this difficult time said, "I never saw anyone take anything so hard as Elvis did with Gladys' death." But he did go on with his life.

While Elvis loved his father dearly, their relationship was not as close as mother and son had been. Gladys had been Elvis' best friend, and Elvis felt betrayed when Vernon married Dee Stanley in 1960. Elvis didn't attend the wedding. No one could take the place of Gladys. When Vernon and his new wife returned to

It's funny, she never really wanted anything fancy. She stayed the same all the way through the whole thing. I wish, you know, there's a lot of things happened since she passed away that I wish she could've been around to see.

—Elvis

• • • •

—Photo courtesy of Linda Everett.

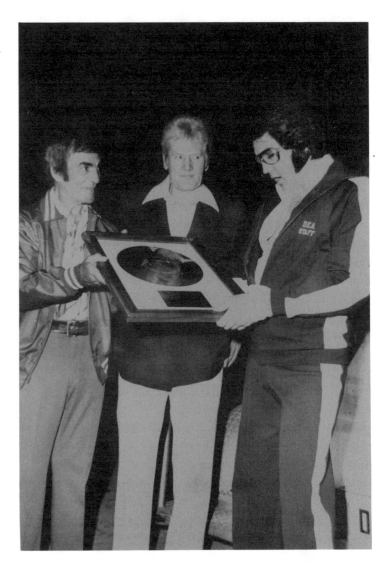

Memphis, Elvis told Dee, "I will treat you with respect and kindness but I want you to remember three things. Number one: You will never replace my mother. Number two: Graceland is not your home. Number three: Don't ever exploit the Presley name."

Vernon and Dee moved into a home at 1266 Dolan, which adjoined the Graceland property. Although Elvis never fully accepted Dee Stanley as his stepmother, he treated her respectfully throughout her seventeen-year marriage to Vernon. When Vernon announced he planned to divorce Dee, Elvis gave her one hundred thousand dollars to leave his father's home.

While Elvis was never fond of his stepmother, he treated her three boys as his own younger brothers. When they first arrived at Graceland he welcomed them with warm hugs. Then he bought presents for them, three of every toy in the department store. Elvis always provided whatever they needed.

Vernon worked as Elvis' financial manager, a responsibility he had accepted with Elvis' first hint of wealth. At the age of 39, Vernon quit his job and switched from earning near minimum wage to watching over an income and expenditures of millions. It was a challenging task. Vernon had to adjust to no longer being the breadwinner and decision maker in the family. He was as frugal as Elvis was spendthrift. Each day Vernon walked from his home to his office in the backyard of Graceland. He worked loyally on his son's behalf until his own death in 1979.

At Graceland, Elvis provided a home to many of his family. His grandmother had lived with the Presleys since moving with them from Tupelo. As a child, Elvis had nicknamed her "Dodger." The name stuck. For several years following Gladys' death, Dodger assumed the role of the woman of the house. Elvis provided for her every need. She had a fear of hospitals and Elvis made sure she was never hospitalized. Whatever she needed was brought to

Daddy just can't adjust. He's gone from handling twenty-five dollars a week to . . . . I've averaged $3 million a year since I was eighteen years old . . . and Daddy goes shopping and comes back with a $3 tie.

—Elvis

• • • •

her. Dodger died at Graceland in 1980 at the age of ninety, and was buried in the Meditation Garden with her son, daughter-in-law, and grandson.

Vernon's sister, Delta Mae Biggs, lost her husband in 1966. She moved into Graceland. Soon she was in charge of the housekeeping and grocery budget of the household. Aunt Delta still resides in Graceland. After the house was opened for tours, she continued as the housekeeper. She supervised the cleaning crews and personally chose the decorations on the dining room table (flowers, placemats and candles), which were frequently changed. Fans sometimes see her sitting outside with her dog, Edmund II.

Aunt Nash (Vernon's other sister) and her husband, Earl, lived at Elvis' Circle G Ranch in Walls, Mississippi. Earl worked as a guard there. After the ranch was sold, they moved to Graceland and lived in a trailer on the estate. Elvis gave Earl work caring for the grounds. While living there, Aunt Nash chose to become an ordained minister in the Assembly of God Church. Soon after her ordination, she founded a church in Walls. It had a humble beginning, starting in a rented house. Elvis bought land for a church to be built on. He gave his Aunt Nash his gold plated piano from the music room at Graceland and told her that if the piano was too large, she should sell it and buy one she could use.

Elvis' Aunt Lorraine (who was married to Gladys' brother, Travis) has said, "Elvis took good care of all of his family. He gave Travis and me a down payment on our home when we moved from Graceland, as well as providing Travis and other family members with good jobs. After Travis died, Elvis called me and said, 'Aunt Lorraine, you have worked hard all your life and now I'm gonna retire you so you can rest and enjoy life.' He made provisions for me in his will when he passed away."

Travis' and Lorraine's son, Billy Smith, worked for Elvis as his valet. He and his wife, Jo, lived in a trailer behind Graceland. Of all of his cousins, Billy was perhaps the closest to him. Billy has said, "Elvis was very close to his family. He made as many jobs available as possible for as many members of his family as he could. Some of them worked at the gate, some in the yard, some traveled with him on tours, and others worked in his office. Those who were unable to work for him received help from Elvis whenever they were in need." It is said that Billy was with Elvis for nearly eighteen hours a day toward the end of Elvis' life. Billy and Jo played racquetball with Elvis in the early morning hours of August 16, 1977.

He gave me a chance to see and do things I would never have done. Friends of Elvis' became a family. They had to because they saw each other all the time.

—Billy Smith

• • • •

Harold Loyd, Elvis' cousin, worked as a security guard for Elvis. Today, he works for the estate in the Automobile Museum. Harold wrote in his book, "Elvis tried very hard to help his relatives, but some of them never showed any appreciation no matter how many times he tried. He did not owe any of us anything. He did many things for me, such as giving me a job, a new truck in 1974, money when I needed it, and most of all he trusted me which means more to me than all the money in the world. I knew if I really needed help I could get it. I never went to him or Vernon for help and was turned down. I never went to them for help unless I needed it and they knew this."

Vester Presley (Vernon's brother), was Elvis' double uncle; he had married Gladys' sister, Clettes. The two families had always been particularly close. Vester had helped Vernon build the two-room house Elvis was born in. They lived near each other in Tupelo, and after Vernon moved his family to Memphis, Vester and his family followed. Before Elvis moved into Graceland, he hired Vester to work as a guard while the stone wall was being built. It was a position that would last more than thirty years.

Elvis said to Vester and the other guards, "Be good to all my fans. They are the ones who put me on the hill." The guards became a personal key to Elvis, because they knew where he was and what he was doing. And they were open, and friendly. Sometimes, they would carry cameras up the long driveway to take pictures of the house for the fans. Elvis encouraged the guards to let small groups through the gates when he was away. For many years, they operated tours of the grounds, carrying as many as their small pink Jeep could carry. Elvis often came down to the gate to sign autographs. The guards kept the fans informed so they might be there at the right time. Through the guards, many fans were allowed to be a part of Elvis Presley's life. In turn, they were treated as celebrities. Vester is one of the most photographed men in the world.

In fact, most of Elvis' family have become well-known among Elvis' fans. Elvis provided for many of them while he was alive and they too are appreciative of the many fans that made it possible.

Elvis sits around and jokes just like one of us, and when he asks me to do anything, he always calls me mister. Why, you would think he was working for us instead of the other way round.

—Big Barnie Smith/Graceland guard.

•　•　•　•

THE WOMEN IN HIS LIFE

*W*hen Elvis was young, and his career was just beginning, the question most often asked of him was, "Elvis, are you in love?" The media were always curious about the women he was dating and wanted to know whether he planned to marry. For many years he confessed to dating different women and not feeling prepared for a permanent relationship. But marriage was something he felt was very sacred, and he wanted it in his own life, when he felt ready.

He once said in an interview, "Maybe I could fall in love and marry someday soon. But I'm not sure whether I've met the right girl or not. Trouble is, time passes too quickly in this business. I'm twenty-eight, but I sure don't feel that old. I've been working so hard I haven't had time to get serious over a girl. When I marry though, it'll be just for one time only."

He was America's most eligible bachelor. Few women could resist his charm and good looks. And Elvis loved women. Early in his career he dated Memphis girls and Hollywood starlets. He was torn between the hometown girls his mother would approve of and the glamorous stars of show business. A lot has been said of his intimate affairs, but only a few women were involved in lengthy relationships with Elvis. Most are still very loyal to him.

Since he skyrocketed to fame, the twenty-four year old Memphian has managed to avoid entanglements with the same dexterity of a kid stealing watermelons through a barbed wire fence.

—Reese Wells/newspaper reporter
March 1960

· · · ·

In the early days at Graceland, Elvis had parties nearly every night. He had a large group of friends that he hung around with — his buddies and his girls. In particular, there were five girls that were a part of his crowd. Most often they were part of the group, not necessarily dates, but female friends. Arlene Cogan Bradley recalls, "It was all so innocent. He played the piano and sang almost every night. Even then his voice was so powerful, and he didn't share it with the world until much later. He had an incredible sense of humor and sometimes I'd leave Graceland hurting from having laughed so hard. All he cared about was for everyone else. He was the most giving person I ever knew."

People have said I was lucky to have known Elvis Presley. I say no; I wasn't lucky. I was blessed.
—Arlene Cogan Bradley

• • • •

Elvis had his friends, but he also had his girlfriends. One of Elvis' early girlfriends was Anita Wood, the hostess of George Klein's "Top 10 Dance Party." One of Elvis' first gifts to her was a sapphire and diamond ring, given to her in August 1957. For Christmas he gave her a toy poodle named "Little Bit." Elvis and Anita spent a lot of time together whenever he was in Memphis and it was rumored they would marry. While some blamed Colonel Parker for insisting Elvis stay single, Anita maintains they simply drifted apart. She said, "Elvis was very shy when I first met him. I was definitely his girl in those days but the trouble was we were never alone. He always seemed to want to be part of a crowd. Gradually, I saw him change, even more as the months passed in Hollywood. Soon, I didn't feel comfortable with him anymore. I admit I cried when he went to Germany, but by then I had made up my mind that I would not marry him."

The move to Germany was difficult for Elvis. He was grieving the loss of his mother and, at the same time, trying to adjust to a life totally foreign to him. Gladys had always encouraged and comforted him. Now, since he had to manage without her, he moved his friends and family to Germany with him.

Priscilla Beaulieu captured Elvis' attention at their very first meeting. She was young — fourteen — beautiful, and American. Elvis soon began confiding in her. He talked about his mother and shared his feelings of loss and despair. Priscilla listened and consoled him. She liked him for his boyish vulnerability, not because he was a teen-age idol. They were together nearly every night in Germany. For Christmas, he gave her a gold wrist watch with a diamond set on the face. That gift was the first of many in a love affair that would last for years. Just a few months later Elvis was discharged from the Army and returned to the States. But he didn't forget Priscilla.

The newspapers and magazines called her "the girl he left behind." She was photographed writing a letter to her sweetheart. Elvis telephoned her. Two years later Elvis persuaded Priscilla's father to let her visit him. Since she was only sixteen, this was not an easy feat.

Priscilla flew into Los Angeles and stayed with Elvis in his newly purchased Bel Air home. Almost immediately he arranged a shopping trip. Priscilla once said he bought her more dresses in two weeks than she had seen in sixteen years. Elvis took Priscilla to Las Vegas and transformed her appearance into that of a woman. He bought her glamorous dresses and arranged for a hairdresser to complete the new look. Now he was ready to introduce her to the nightlife. They went to shows and played the gaming tables. Priscilla had never played blackjack, but Elvis gave her five hundred dollars to learn. Two weeks passed and she returned to Germany. Priscilla said, "The thing I remember most about those early days is that it was all so much fun because Elvis was a boy at heart. He was practically bursting at the seams with happiness and the joy of his success. He was always joking, always doing fun things. Every night was a party. Our relationship found solid ground and Elvis admitted he loved me."

I was shocked at how ordinary he was, how warm and friendly and open.

—Priscilla Presley

• • • •

—Photo courtesy of
AP Wide World Photos

Nine months later Priscilla visited Elvis at Graceland for Christmas. Elvis' present to her was a puppy. He had decided Priscilla should live with him. Two months later Priscilla returned to Memphis and enrolled in Immaculate Conception High School. Elvis provided for her every need. He frequently took her shopping for clothes. She drove his car and had whatever material possessions she might want. For her high school graduation in 1963, Elvis bought her a red Corvair. In December 1966, Elvis gave her a three and a half carat diamond engagement ring. They were married in May 1967. The following Christmas, he gave her a Fleetwood Cadillac limousine.

On February 1, 1968, Lisa Marie was born. Elvis now had a child who would have the very best that money could buy. There was no limit to the gifts he would buy her. Her birthdays were lavish celebrations with Lisa receiving toys most children only dream about. When she was just six, Elvis bought her a golf cart to ride in around the estate. Later, he bought her a pony and encouraged her to ride through the front door of Graceland so Dodger could see it. Needless to say, his grandmother wasn't amused. Nothing was off limits where his daughter was concerned.

When Lisa was eight, Elvis bought her a diamond ring and a mink coat. Priscilla insisted Elvis return them. Though she wanted Lisa to understand the value of money and the rewards of hard work, she found it difficult to dampen his enthusiasm for indulging his only child. She once said, "Elvis is hard to handle as a father. He slips her potato chips and lets her stay up. He gives her five dollars for the tooth fairy, after I had just given her fifty cents. But he can't help it, he loves her so. Anyhow, one can't expect Elvis Presley to know what the tooth fairy is paying these days." Both of the women in Elvis' life had virtually anything they wanted. Elvis would return home from a trip with extravagant gifts for them.

Many of his friends have said these were the happiest years of Elvis' life. He adored Lisa Marie, and reveled in her every accomplishment. But Priscilla tired of life behind the walls of Graceland. In 1972 she moved into her own home in California, taking Lisa with her. Priscilla and Elvis were divorced in 1973. For the rest of his life, he only saw Lisa for visitations during the summer or holidays.

Any divorce is painful. For Elvis, it was devastating. It pained him to lose close contact with Lisa, and his traditional upbringing had instilled in him the belief that marriage was a lifetime commitment. Priscilla had shared his life for many years before they married and had known his lifestyle. He thought nothing had changed. It was humiliating to be adored by millions of women but rejected by his own wife. Furthermore, he was in the public eye and so everyone, it seemed, knew about their personal problems. Be it a blessing or a curse, Elvis' career was at its peak.

While Elvis and Priscilla struggled to reach a legal settlement, he staged "Aloha From Hawaii." It was the most extravagant production attempted by any entertainer. Elvis rose to the occasion. He satisfied his audience by singing his popular songs. But there was a maturity about him that was unfamiliar.

He sang songs of weary resignation and lost love. The songs "I'm So Lonesome I Could Cry," "I Can't Stop Loving You," "It's Over," and "You Gave Me a Mountain," reflected his pain.

It was during this difficult period while Elvis and Priscilla were separated that Linda Thompson met Elvis. She once said, "I met Elvis at a time when he really needed someone to be with." Linda was fun-loving and spontaneous. She brought a new dimension to Elvis' life.

For their first Christmas together Elvis gave Linda a mink coat. He bought her thousands of dollars worth of jewelry and gave her money for whatever clothes or other items she wanted. In May 1976, he surprised her with a Lincoln Continental Mark IV. Although she spent most of her time with him at his home or on tour, he bought her a house near Graceland. Elvis accepted her family as his own and hired her brother, Sam Thompson, as a security guard. He paid for her parents' home.

One of Linda's favorite stories is about their dog, Getlo, a beautiful red chow which Elvis adored. Occasionally, the dog traveled to Las Vegas with them. The dog became ill and a Memphis veterinarian diagnosed a rare kidney ailment. Elvis leased a Lear jet to fly Getlo, Linda, and one of her girlfriends to Boston. Getlo was treated at one of the country's finest veterinary hospitals and returned to Memphis. Sadly, she died a few months later. Linda recalls, "For some time after that, whenever Elvis thought of Getlo, it would bring tears to his eyes."

Linda and Elvis broke up in December 1976. Linda has said, "Once Elvis has touched your life, you were never the same again. No one will ever replace him, not for me or for anybody who knew him. We had some good times together and I believe I helped him over the pain and hurt of his divorce. I loved Elvis and believe he loved me."

Shortly after his breakup with Linda, Elvis was introduced to Ginger Alden. He took her to Las Vegas for his engagement at the Hilton. While there he bought her a white-on-white Lincoln Mark IV. When he and Ginger flew back to Memphis, he had the car driven home. Concerned that Ginger might be without a car for a few days, he immediately bought her a Cadillac Seville.

Elvis was fond of Ginger's family. He installed a swimming pool at her mother's home and paid for extensive landscaping. Mrs. Alden was in the process of divorcing her husband. Ginger said, "Elvis was disturbed our home life was not as pleasant as we would

We think of how fortunate we were to have known him, to have shared so much of his life with him.
—Linda Thompson

• • • •

like for it to be and there were differences between my mother and father." He involved himself in the divorce, assisting Mrs. Alden with attorneys' fees. Elvis offered to buy the Aldens a home closer to Graceland but they refused. Instead, Elvis paid Mr. Alden the equity in their home so Mrs. Alden could keep the property. He intended to pay the mortgage off.

His jeweler, Lowell Hays, remembers when Elvis ordered a diamond ring for Ginger. "The first call came around 7 A.M. I told him what he wanted was impossible and he told me, 'Look, I do all my business with you and when I need something special, I need it special. I want this diamond tonight and I want you to get it for me.' I realized he meant business. I made arrangements to get the diamond he wanted out of my vault in the middle of the night, called my jeweler, and he met me at my store. We put the ring together for him and got it to him about eight in the morning." The ring had an eleven and a half carat diamond. Ginger was Elvis' last girlfriend. After his death she said the ring was an engagement ring. They had planned a Christmas wedding.

Elvis with Ginger.
—Photo courtesy of June Kwiatkowski.

WHAT ARE
FRIENDS FOR?

*W*hen Gladys died, Eddie Fadal, a friend from Waco, Texas, accompanied Elvis from Fort Hood, his Army base, to Graceland. Eddie packed an overnight bag expecting to spend a few days in Memphis. As each day passed, Eddie mentioned he needed to return to his family in Waco. Elvis said. "No way, Eddie, I haven't had a chance to show you Memphis yet." Every time Eddie offered nice excuses to return home, Elvis would say something like, "I haven't shown you where I used to live, or where I went to school, or Sun Studio." Finally, Eddie told him he had to go home because he hadn't brought enough clean clothes.

"Come on, Elvis replied. "We'll take care of that in a hurry." Eddie didn't know what Elvis had in mind but followed him to one of the cars parked outside Graceland. Elvis drove speedily toward downtown Memphis with an expression that said, "Nobody dare try to stop me." He parked the car and they went into Lansky Brothers' Men's Clothing Store.

The Lanskys greeted Elvis enthusiastically. They were good friends and when Elvis visited them, he usually spent a lot of money. This day was no exception. After exchanging greetings Elvis told Eddie, "Pick out a wardrobe here. Get anything you want." Eddie told Elvis he had plenty of clothes at home; he just needed to get back to his family. His pleas fell on deaf ears. Elvis

Elvis with Eddie Fadal.
—Photo courtesy of Eddie Fadal.

opened the door and started walking out. He turned around and told Mr. Lansky, "Give Eddie anything in the store he wants. Give him the whole store if he wants it." Elvis then walked out of the store, went to a shoe shine stall on the sidewalk, and sat down.

Each time Lansky showed Eddie something, Eddie said, "I have that at home, I don't need it. I don't need anything." Finally, Lansky said, "Elvis will get mad if you don't buy something." Eddie picked out a pullover, sport-knit shirt in red. Lansky went to work monogramming Eddie's initials on it. Elvis came back into the store a few moments later.

"Is that all you picked up in this big store?" he said. He went to the counter where the shirts were displayed and began picking one of every color in stock. "Here, put Eddie's initials on all of these," he told Lansky.

Elvis then began searching all the aisles, pulling out things he wanted Eddie to have. He picked out a black mohair suit, a beautiful silk, beige-tone sportcoat, socks, underwear, slacks, and neckties of varied colors.

"Here, bring these out to Graceland tonight and alter them for Eddie," Elvis told Lansky. Eddie continued to protest that he didn't want or need these clothes but Elvis pretended not to hear him. As Elvis drove back to Graceland, he pointed out landmarks and attractions around Memphis. He wouldn't discuss the purchases.

About 7 o'clock that night, just as Elvis had specified, Lansky drove up to the mansion with his tailor, the clothes, and a portable sewing machine. They began taking Eddie's measurements and making the alterations. The work was finished in about an hour and a half, and everything fit perfectly.

"Eddie, put on all those things. I want to see how they fit and how you look in them," Elvis said. Of course, Eddie did and Elvis was pleased beyond description. "Now you gotta stay until I have to be back to Fort Hood. We'll fly back together," Elvis said. And that's what they did about thirty days later.

Elvis demanded a lot from his friends. He wanted them there when he needed them. At times his temper got the better of him. His friends had to wait out his tantrums, knowing he would cool off and quickly forget his outburst. Sometimes he would retreat into his room, and his friends would sit quietly by, for however many hours or days Elvis needed to be alone. They knew Elvis would emerge full of energy, wanting his friends' company for whatever his imagination had dreamed up. He might want to fly to the west coast or rent a movie theater in town, immediately. His friends had to be ready for anything.

Among the few predictable things about Elvis was his loyalty. He cared deeply about his friends and they knew this. If something troubled one of them, Elvis worried about it. He wanted to fix things. J.D. Sumner has said, "You had to keep things from him because if he heard of a need, he tried to fill it."

Felton Jarvis, his last record producer, said, "I owe my life to Elvis. I was getting real sick, had high blood pressure. I waited two years and couldn't get a kidney transplant. I was living on a kidney machine and one day Elvis says, 'I've stayed out of it long enough. I'm gonna see if I can't get you a kidney.' So he called some doctors and six days later I was transplanted. So I owe him an awful lot. He's some kind of man." The operation added eleven years to his life.

Elvis was quick to pull out his checkbook if he thought he could help a friend. When he learned that Jackie Wilson, a fellow entertainer whom Elvis admired, was hospitalized following a heart attack, he sent a check for thirty thousand dollars to his wife to help with medical expenses. In these situations, Elvis insisted on anonymity. His friends have alluded to many other similar stories.

A close friend, Richard Davis, once said, "You can live ten lifetimes and you'll never find another like him. He's got a heart of gold. He'll give you the shirt off his back." This sentiment is expressed by many others who were a part of Elvis' private world.

Elvis' closest friends were called the "Memphis Mafia." Most of them were family or friends from high school who also worked for him. Elvis paid a modest salary but each Christmas gave out a substantial bonus. And he always gave them money if any of them were running short of cash. If they needed several thousand dollars to make a down payment on a house, he provided it. He also bought them expensive gifts: cars, televisions, and stereos. What was bought for one was usually bought for all.

He stuck by me when I needed him most. When RCA wanted to record him live at Madison Square Garden, I was flat on my back with kidney problems. When they asked Elvis and Colonel Parker whether they could record the show, they said, 'Yes, but only if you pay Felton Jarvis as if he were there.' My whole life itself, my home, my jewelry, everything I've got is owed to him.

—Felton Jarvis

• • • •

At times Elvis would forget an important occasion. He usually gave when it was least expected, months before a birthday or holiday. He was a master of spontaneity, particularly when giving "happies," his word for gifts. Elvis enjoyed watching the reactions of his friends to his surprises. They were speechless and unable to say much else beyond "thank you."

He wanted his gifts to be his idea. If someone asked for a car he might not give it to him, unless he sensed that person really needed it. If, instead, someone admired a particular car, Elvis might hand him the keys. Of course, many people learned how to lead Elvis into believing an idea was his, and get what they wanted.

One night George Klein received a call from one of Elvis' friends. "Elvis has to see you now, downtown at the showroom," he said. When George arrived, all of the lights were off. Suddenly, every light was turned on, spotlighting a brand new '68 Cadillac. "Merry Christmas G.K.," Elvis said. "What's fame and fortune if you can't share it with your friends?"

Special occasions brought special gifts. When bodyguard Dick Grob got married, Elvis gave him a small wedding present. Later, as Dick stepped out of the church, he was stunned to find a brand new car waiting for him. Dick said, "I drove to the church in a Volkswagen and left in a Mercury Marquis."

Elvis' automobile-buying sprees made him every salesman's dream. He bought expensive models and he rarely bought just one. One night, while living in Bel Air, he thought that on such a warm night he should be driving a convertible. Elvis and his friends immediately went to a nearby dealership. A black Cadillac convertible caught Elvis' eye and he purchased it for himself. The eight friends with him also left with new cars. Elvis, never forgetting his and his friends' teen-age dreams of having fancy cars, enjoyed making such dreams come true.

In Memphis, Elvis often visited the car dealerships. On Saturday, September 23, 1974, he walked into Schilling Lincoln-Mercury on

Elvis took good care of us.
—Jerry Schilling

• • • •

Elvis showed up about 3 A.M. shopping for cars. He bought thirteen Cadillacs in an hour and a half. The bill came to $168,000. They were Christmas presents for his staff.

—Pat Gilmore,
Memphis Cadillac Dealer.

• • • •

Union Avenue. By Sunday night he had visited the dealership five times. Elvis bought their entire stock of Mark IV's. For sixty thousand dollars he received cars in red, black, aqua, silver, and blue; two had sunroofs. The salesman earned over four thousand dollars in commission. Elvis had bought the cars as gifts for his girlfriend, Linda Thompson; his cousin, Billy Smith; and three friends; Red West, Marty Lacker, and Richard Davis. During this buying spree he also purchased five Cadillacs. He gave them to Vester Presley, Gee Gee Gamble (his cousin's husband and also one of Elvis' aides), and Mrs. Barbara Klein. He kept two for himself.

Madison Cadillac, then located on Union Avenue, was Elvis' favorite Cadillac dealership. He had been loyal to the store since the Fifties. On January 17, 1975, he bought eleven Cadillacs. In July of that year he purchased fourteen. In September he went on another binge and bought cars for his uncle, his cousin, his cousin's husband, and another female friend. That was the last car he would give his uncle Vester — a gold Cadillac Coupe De Ville. Not long afterwards, salesman Bob Brown gave Elvis a plaque for being the "World's Best Car Buyer." Inscribed were the names of thirty-one people to whom Elvis had given a car.

Elvis gave jewelry to everyone in his circle. His jeweler, Lowell Hays, of Memphis, said, "He bought bracelets and necklaces but mainly it was rings. Elvis was a particular shopper. He believed in numbers, in numerology. If he had a particular person he wanted to buy a gift for, he would look in his book and buy what the book said his stone was. He'd find that someone's stone was a star sapphire, a black opal, or a blue sapphire, and he would tell me what kind of ring he needed." A special group wore Elvis' own insignia. A Beverly Hills jeweler custom made the legendary lightning bolt. Speed and efficiency were important to Elvis. The incorporation of the lightning bolt with his motto, T.C.B., meant "Taking Care of Business in a Flash." Only thirteen of these pendants were made, twelve for his friends and one for himself. Then the mold was

Whenever he was in a gift giving mood, he would get a gleam in his eyes that was unmistakable. When he wanted to purchase something to give it away, he wanted it that moment, regardless of the time of day.

—Ed Parker.

• • • •

broken. The men in Elvis' group wore the pendant on chains, and added their own diamonds to the gold ornament.

Elvis also gave gold friendship bracelets to his closest friends; once again only a few were made. The name of the friend was inscribed on the outside, and Elvis' pet name for them was inscribed on the inside. George Klein's bracelet said "Rock'n 50's," Richard Davis' was "Beer Brain," Alan Fortas' was "Hog Ears," Joe Esposito's was "The Brain," and Ed Parker's was "Kahuna." Elvis wore a bracelet that read "Crazy," in reference to his impulsive pranks.

One of the pranks that earned Elvis his nickname was staged at Christmas. Everyone had become accustomed to Elvis' extravagant holiday gifts and the room was filled with anticipation as Elvis started distributing envelopes. They were certain the envelopes contained money or keys to new automobiles. Instead they found two-dollar gift certificates for McDonald's. As he watched the disappointed faces, Elvis announced that it had been a lean year. Eventually he let out a laugh and began distributing the real gifts: envelopes filled with money.

Elvis' employees, even those who were not on the daily work schedule, were often surprised by his generous spirit. George Coleman, his electrician, came to Graceland whenever Elvis had electrical needs. Late one night, Elvis called him to repair a problem with a light, saying it might be the light bulb. George climbed out of bed, muttering about having to disturb his sleep to handle something so simple. At Graceland he found something remarkable, a brand new blue pick-up truck, complete with new tools, waiting for him.

Mary Jenkins, who worked as Elvis' maid and later as his cook, experienced Elvis' generosity many times. She had been on the job for just three months when she received word that Elvis wanted to see her and another employee outside. It was an unusual request, and they wondered if they might be fired. They hadn't dreamed they would see four brand new automobiles lined up in the driveway.

Elvis' philosophy was, I've been lucky so I want to share with my friends.

—Jerry Schilling

• • • •

Elvis said to the cook, "Daisy, would you like this Buick? It's yours." She was so excited she ran to Elvis and lifted him up off the ground. Mary recalls, Elvis started laughing so hard she didn't think he would ever stop. Finally he said to Mary, "Would you like to have a car?" He gave her a white Ford. The other cars were for the night shift employees. Elvis bought cars for all of those who worked in the house.

In the fourteen years that Mary worked for Elvis he bought her six cars, including the Ford, three Cadillacs, a Mercury, and a Pontiac. He even bought a car for her friend and "play brother." "Willie, if I can give you a car, then surely you can take me riding in it," Elvis said as he handed him the keys. Elvis, Mary, and another girl who worked at Graceland jumped into the Cadillac.

As they were driving around, Mary mentioned she liked one of the houses they had passed. "Mary, why didn't you tell me you want a house?" Elvis said. "Talk to a Realtor, get her to give you a book, and pick one out." A few days later she told him she'd found two that she liked in the real estate book. He instructed her, "Call the Realtor and tell her we want to look at these." Three real estate agents arrived the next day and Elvis drove with them to look at houses.

Mary fell in love with the first house they looked at. Elvis said to the agents, "Get the papers ready!" He paid cash for the house and the year's taxes. "I don't want you to bring a piece of furniture with you," he then said to Mary. "I want to furnish it all. I want to put down new carpet. I want to have the draperies made and I want to buy new furniture.

That night he left for California and didn't return to Memphis for many months. Many felt that if he could buy her a house, surely she could furnish it. And she did. When Elvis returned home he asked, "Now Mary, you didn't buy any furniture, did you?" Mary admitted she had.

"I asked you not to."

"But you bought the house," Mary answered.

"That ain't nothing. I wanted to buy the furniture too. I wanted to do everything."

When Elvis found out that Mary was trying to collect money for her church, he made a large donation. Later he bought a pew for the church and had his and Mary's names put on it. He did a lot for Mary, and he took care of all of his employees. Mary recalls he even paid one employee's tuition through college.

Marion Cocke, Elvis' nurse at Baptist Hospital, received a shiny white Pontiac Grand Prix while he was a patient. Elvis made arrangements for its purchase and told Ms. Cocke to look out the window as he handed her the keys. When she went out to the parking lot to look at her new car, he stood at the window smiling. He also bought her a mink coat and a three carat diamond cross.

One friend who received a surprise gift from Elvis is now the mayor of Shelby County (of which Memphis is the county seat). Mayor Bill Morris shared a similar background with Elvis; his father knew the Presleys in Tupelo and his wife had graduated from Humes High School with Elvis. But their strongest tie was a mutual love for law enforcement. After his duties as sheriff ended, Bill Morris visited Graceland one Christmas Eve. He was sitting in the den when one of the guys came in and said, "Elvis wants to see you outside." There was a brand new black Mercedes car in front of the house.

"Do you see my new car?" said Elvis.

"Yeah, that's a fantastic car. I understand the Mercedes is a great automobile."

"You'd better like it because it's yours," Elvis replied. "Get in and I'll drive you around and show you how to operate this thing." As they started driving through the gates of Graceland onto Highway 51, he turned on the radio. Elvis' song, "I'll Be Home For Christmas," was playing.

Mayor Morris has said, "I'd lived through very humble early years and had never had anything of my own to speak of, and certainly

I was privileged to be a friend of Elvis Presley. I can think of no greater hero in our city, no greater name, no greater contributor to the welfare of more people.

—Bill Morris/
Shelby County Mayor

• • • •

Elvis receiving one of the gifts he liked best—a sheriff's badge.
—Photo courtesy of Janelle McComb.

no one had ever given me anything. But when he said, 'that car is yours,' I knew he was serious. For one of the few times in my life I was speechless. It was hard to even say thank you. You don't just say thank you, but to him that's all he wanted, and he didn't even want that."

"Elvis was always giving something to someone," drummer D. J. Fontana recalled. D.J. worked with Elvis until 1968 and they remained friends throughout Elvis' life. D.J. said, "He gave so much away. Rings, watches, houses, cars. He'd give a car to anybody that looked like they needed an automobile. He gave so much to charity and never bragged about it."

He got a charge out of having me guess how to turn on the wipers.
—Bill Morris

• • • •

Elvis came to one recording session wearing a brand new horseshoe diamond ring that was so bright, the light reflected off of it onto every wall. D.J. said, "Boy, that ole ring's shining pretty good, Elvis. Look at that thing."

"Here, why don't you wear it. When we get through tonight or in the morning, you can give it back to me," Elvis replied. D.J. wore the ring all during the session. When they finished he walked up to Elvis and said, "Here's your ring back."

"Shoot! Keep that thing."

"Well you might need it."

"Yeah, when I go broke I'll call you."

A few years after D.J. quit the band, he saw Elvis again. "He had a whole acre of rings on. I said, 'Boy, them are pretty rings.' Elvis said, 'No, you got me once. Not these.'"

J.D. Sumner and Elvis were life-long friends. When Elvis' mother died, J.D. sang with the Blackwood Brothers at her funeral. Many years later, when Elvis died, Vernon entrusted him with choosing the minister and music for Elvis' funeral. He brought in James Blackwood, and The Statesmen. J.D. and The Stamps sang "How Great Thou Art."

J.D. remembers, "Elvis was the most humble man, the most giving man. Generous doesn't even begin to describe him." Elvis gave J.D. a limousine in 1976. At the time, Elvis was recording an album at Graceland but was not satisfied with the work. He called off the recording session. In the course of arranging transportation for all of the musicians and vocalists, he gave his limousine to J.D.

There were some items that J.D. couldn't accept. Elvis tried to buy him a $350,000 airplane. He felt J.D. deserved greater comfort than the tour bus they often used. J.D. responded, "Elvis, I couldn't afford to park it, much less fly it." Then Elvis offered to buy J.D. and his wife a condominium in Memphis. J.D. refused this offer as well. He enjoyed his home in Nashville.

The gift which pleased J.D. most was a diamond ring. During a concert, Elvis took off his brand new TCB diamond ring and gave it to J.D. Elvis had personally designed the ring with a ten carat white diamond center stone. Lightning bolts decorated both sides and TCB was spelled on the top. The ring was valued at forty thousand dollars but the sentiment behind the gift was priceless.

Elvis also gave gifts to other performers on his tours, particularly when he was impressed with their loyalty to him. Once, on stage in Virginia, members of the Sweet Inspirations were offended by a joke Elvis made. Elvis had never liked fish, and couldn't tolerate its smell. The women in the group had eaten fish for dinner, and Elvis kidded them about it. For the first time in his career, his vocalists walked off the stage. Myrna Smith was the only member of the group to stay on stage with him. Elvis was so appreciative of her expression of loyalty, he gave her a twenty-five thousand dollar diamond ring immediately after the show. The following morning he presented her with a new Cadillac El Dorado. By that evening the others had apologized to Elvis and returned to the stage.

Other entertainers also received gifts from Elvis. He once gave Sammy Davis Jr. a diamond ring. Lowell Hays remembers: "Elvis came down and sat at the dining room table and said, 'Where is it?' I gave it to him, he slipped it on his finger and looked at it and said, 'God, won't Sammy love this!' Then Elvis asked how much

Was he my friend? Did he entertain? Did he give something to the world of entertainment? Yes, on all three accounts.

—Sammy Davis Jr.

• • • •

he owed me. I told him fifty-five thousand dollars. He said, 'You gotta be kidding.' No Elvis, it's got an eleven and one-half carat diamond in it. 'Well, all right,' Elvis smiled, then looked at me with that lopsided grin and said, 'Now I want to do something for you Lowell. What do you want?'"

Nancy Sinatra, who had appeared in the film "Speedway" with Elvis, received a full page ad for her Las Vegas show from Elvis. He presented her with the engraving plates. Elvis gave comedian Redd Foxx an expensive gold watch. While attending Vikki Carr's show in Las Vegas he joined her on stage. He had given her a diamond ring and the two showed off their rings to the audience.

Once Elvis tried to give a gift to Vice President Spiro Agnew. He arranged a meeting with him in Palm Springs with the intention of giving him a gold inlaid revolver, worth about two thousand dollars. The Vice President refused the present because as an elected official he felt that accepting the gift would not be proper.

Colonel Parker was offered Elvis' most expensive gift, a $1.2 million airplane. The aircraft, which seated twelve people, was equipped with a stereo system, a bar, and a flight phone. Colonel Parker was overwhelmed but said he couldn't accept the gift. It was too extravagant.

For Elvis, nothing was too extravagant. His family and friends deserved the best. Red West, his bodyguard and high school friend, once speculated that perhaps Elvis gave so much to those around him because he couldn't give to the person he wanted so much to have everything—his mother. His uncle, Vester, reasoned that because Elvis couldn't enjoy ordinary activities he could enjoy making others happy. Mary Jenkins said it simply, "He just got a kick out of doing for people."

Elvis was something that comes along about once in two thousand years. I remember the night Frank Sinatra had a party for his daughter, Nancy, after her Las Vegas Show. The room was crammed with stars, the biggest ones. But, when Elvis came in, everything stopped. All eyes were on him.

—Jerry Schilling.

• • • •

Mennie Person showing off her
surprise gift.
—Photo courtesy of the
Mississippi Valley Collection,
Memphis State University.

THE HALLMARK OF A LEGEND

*I*magine visiting a car dealership one Sunday night. You're browsing, not planning to buy anything. A limousine in the parking lot catches your eye, and as you're admiring it, a voice asks if you like it. You turn to find Elvis standing there.

That's exactly what happened to Mennie Person, a bank teller in Memphis. When Mennie told Elvis she liked the car he said, "That one's mine but I'll buy you one." He then took her arm, led her to a fleet of Cadillacs and told her to pick one out. She chose a gold-and-white El Dorado, and Elvis told the dealer to put it on his list.

As Elvis handed her the keys to the Cadillac, Mennie said "Tomorrow's my birthday. This will be the greatest birthday present I ever had."

Elvis asked for his checkbook. "Honey, here's twenty-five hundred dollars for your birthday."

Elvis once bought Cadillacs and Lincolns for members of the police department in Denver, Colorado. Captain Jerry Kennedy and his wife; Police Doctor Gerald Starkey, Detective Ron Pietrofeso, and Organized Crime Strike Force Member Robert Cantwell received new cars. These men had assisted with security during some of Elvis' previous concerts. Denver's police chief, Art Dill, refused Elvis' offer of an automobile. He said, "I will say

He could remember when he was growing up poor, and he and his mamma and daddy would go to an automobile dealer's and look through the glass at the cars.

—Joe Esposito

• • • •

it was difficult to refuse. Mr. Presley seemed hurt when I had to tell him no, but I explained my position to him and thanked him for his offer." The police chief approved acceptance of the gifts by the other officers because they weren't working on Elvis' security at the time Elvis purchased the automobiles.

In the book *Elvis: What Happened?* there is a story in which Elvis is said to have left Denver abruptly, after one of these officers told Elvis he knew he was abusing a prescribed drug. The officer concerned, Robert Cantwell, disputes that story. He remembers that Elvis became angered at a remark he made when Elvis gave him the car. According to his own account, Cantwell told Elvis, "I've never gotten anything for nothing." Elvis became very upset and said, "I don't want you questioning why I gave it to you. I gave you the car because you treat me like I'm a person, not like I'm Elvis Presley. I think it would be best if I left right now."

Memphis had become somewhat accustomed to Elvis' buying sprees, but this was something Denver had not experienced. The media loved the news story. One broadcaster jokingly said on television, "Elvis, if you're listening, I could use a car." J.D. Sumner recalls Elvis' reaction. J.D. was sitting with him in his suite and Elvis very calmly said, "Give me the phone." He called the dealer and immediately had a new black Cadillac Seville delivered to the television station. When the broadcaster stepped out of the studio, a brand new car was waiting for him, courtesy of Elvis Presley.

The man made $4 billion—I didn't say million—in his life and gave away over half of it.

—J.D. Sumner

• • • •

Mennie Person happened to be at the car dealership at the same time Elvis was on a buying spree. The television announcer happened to make a remark that Elvis heard. Elvis' gifts to her and the broadcaster are the hallmark of a legend. His impromptu gifts of cars, jewelry, and money are as much a part of Elvis lore as his music or movies.

Even those who knew him best were unprepared when Elvis impulsively made a decision. On one very rare occasion, Elvis took a commercial flight to California. He called Jerry Schilling and said, "I'm traveling by myself. I don't want anybody to know where I'm at. I'm coming in on flight so and so." Jerry recalls thinking, "This is so strange. I didn't know he knew flight numbers because we always did all of that for him."

"Will you meet me at the airport about 2 A.M.?" Elvis said. "You can get the limousine driver we normally use. Tell him not to say anything." Jerry was allowed to go right up to the plane. Elvis was the last one off. He was carrying a small cardboard box. When Jerry asked him what was in the box Elvis said, "It's my luggage."

The next day Elvis declared, "We need to go to Washington. I want to see President Nixon."

"I have to go to work in the morning," Jerry said.

"No problem. I'll get a Lear jet to fly you back."

"The other planes go just as fast. I can't take the day off from work."

"OK, I'll go by myself then." Elvis said. Jerry didn't want Elvis to fly around the country by himself so he told him, "Forget it. I'll go with you." They had no money. Elvis had a credit card. It was Sunday night and it was very difficult to cash a check. Finally, their limousine driver remembered someone at the Beverly Hilton Hotel. They were able to get a check cashed for five hundred dollars.

They preboarded the plane and as people got on, Elvis spoke to them. He started talking to a soldier who was returning from Viet Nam. The next thing Jerry knew, Elvis was poking him in the ribs. "Where's that money?"

"What money?" Jerry asked.

"The money we just got."

"But that's all we got!"

He had a feeling for anyone who was poor.

—Joe Esposito

• • • •

President Nixon admiring Elvis' cufflinks.

—Photo courtesy of Linda Everett.

Elvis had the power over people's imaginations that would enable him to obtain high office.

—Richard M. Nixon

• • • •

"You don't understand," Elvis said. "This man is going home for Christmas. He's been in Viet Nam." Elvis gave the soldier the whole five hundred dollars.

Every friend of Elvis' has a story or two about his unpredictable nature. Eddie Fadal recalled a time Elvis drove him to downtown Memphis. A red light forced him to stop. Elvis spotted an old man seated on the corner. He was obviously blind and held a tin cup with yellow pencils. Not saying a word to Eddie about what he was thinking, Elvis circled the block. When he returned to the corner, the light was red again. Elvis immediately stopped the car, put on the emergency brake, and got out. He walked over to the man with the cup of pencils and Eddie saw him drop several one hundred dollar bills into the cup. Elvis hurried back to the car and drove on to Beale Street, not saying a word to Eddie about his impromptu gift.

His cousin, Billy Smith, told of an incident that occurred shortly after Elvis started earning big money. "Elvis went up to a newspaper stand and told the vendor he wanted a paper. Elvis pulled out a hundred dollar bill and the man said, 'I don't have the change for anything that big.' Elvis told him, 'Well, then just keep the change.' The man was ecstatic. He tried to give Elvis all the papers, but Elvis kept refusing. He could only read one."

Joe Esposito remembers a similar incident. He told this story: "One night a couple of weeks before Christmas we'd been to his mother's grave and were driving along a Memphis street when we saw an old, black man, pushing a cart. He was selling junk. Elvis said, 'Stop a minute.' We stopped. He jumped out and handed the man all the money he had on him. 'Merry Christmas,' he said. I don't think the man knew who'd given him the money. It happened so fast."

Elvis appreciated the simple generosity of other people and rewarded them in his own way. One such incident occurred at a pay phone. Elvis was driving his limousine to Nashville with Felton Jarvis, his record producer, when they stopped to make a call. Felton stepped out of the car and realized he didn't have any change. He asked a man standing there if he might have a dime. Elvis watched the man reach in his pocket and give Felton the coin. He told Felton to get the man's name and address. A few weeks later Elvis sent the man a thank you note with the incredible news he had paid off the man's mortgage on his home.

One friend who knew Elvis throughout his life has said that much about Elvis is exaggerated. The temptation was to embellish Elvis stories to enhance the super hero image. Stories of his generosity were no exception and sometimes the amounts of his gifts were inflated. A prevalent rumor was that Elvis financed a new church building for the First Assembly of God, the church he had attended as a teen-ager. Reverend James Hamill, the pastor, remembered a donation of two thousand dollars by Elvis to the

Elvis was a pushover when it came to the downtrodden, the sad story of the underdog.

—Ed Parker.

• • • •

building fund. It was a generous amount, but not enough to build a church.

Because Elvis did not seek publicity for his acts of kindness, many events were not reported. Some of the accounts did not surface until after his death. In 1976 Elvis donated seven thousand dollars to the Los Angeles Police Department with the stipulation that there was to be no publicity. Word of his arrival spread throughout the building as secretaries and police officers tried to get a glimpse of him. According to one officer, a girl stepped out of her office, saw Elvis, screamed, and slammed the door. But in spite of the internal excitement, the department kept the donation secret.

The media learned of the event in September 1977, when the Los Angeles Police Department honored Elvis at the convention for the International Association of Chiefs of Police. Elvis' presentation to Police Chief Edward M. Davis was the largest single donation made to the organization and was used to buy Christmas toys for poor children and uniforms for the LAPD marching band.

On many occasions Elvis gave when he read of a need in the newspaper. An account of a female student in trouble at Elvis' Humes High School, caught his attention. Her parents had moved away from Memphis and she wanted to finish her education at Humes. The Board of Education insisted she pay tuition. Elvis sent her a check to cover all costs. Then the Board reconsidered. When she no longer needed to pay tuition, she brought the money back to Graceland. Elvis told her to keep it.

Years later he read of an elderly black woman in need of a wheelchair. She lived on a meager pension and had used her wheelchair for so many years it had deteriorated. Her friends had started a fund to buy her a new one. Elvis bought and personally delivered a brand new electric model, and then gave her a check for two hundred dollars. He also sent a check for one thousand

I saw him do things for kids that he'd die if he knew I was telling you about. He sent five thousand dollars to a hospital for retarded children in Fort Worth, Texas. He read in a newspaper during the four days that we were in that city that a hospital needed money to buy games and toys for those kids.

—Nevada Hotel Owner

• • • •

dollars to a Memphis man who was hospitalized following a serious automobile accident.

In Los Angeles, Elvis learned of a police officer who had lost a leg. The officer had nine children to support and his plight was broadcast over the radio. Elvis sent a check for one thousand dollars to the newscaster for the policeman. When Elvis read an article about a summer camp in New Orleans that had been vandalized, he sent a check to the camp to cover their losses.

Elvis responded to fund-raising drives on television. A telethon in Los Angeles received a phone call from Colonel Parker, and probably first assumed it was a prank call. Parker said Elvis would donate half of the final amount of the tote board. His contribution was eighty-five thousand dollars.

On another occasion Elvis' pledge brought him the opportunity to poke fun at some of his friends. J.D. Sumner and The Stamps were guests at a telethon for a Las Vegas church. Elvis was watching the telethon when the minister asked J.D. if Elvis might come by. J.D. didn't expect Elvis to watch or to visit the telethon. He told the minister he would jump in the swimming pool if he did. Elvis saw his chance. He called the station and offered twenty-five hundred dollars if J.D. and The Stamps jumped in the pool. He then pledged another thousand dollars if the minister jumped in. J.D. and his partners dove into the pool. The minister had to be thrown in. And Elvis sent them a check for thirty-five hundred dollars.

Usually when Elvis contributed to a fund-raising drive, there was a more formal ceremony. In June 1968, Elvis donated fifty-thousand dollars to the Motion Picture Relief Fund, an organization which operates a home and hospital for indigent people of the film industry. Elvis had earlier donated seventy-five thousand dollars to the cause, making Elvis' contribution the largest single gift in the fifteen-year existence of the fund. Barbara Stanwyck, Frank Sinatra,

It was his sense of humor that stuck in my mind. He liked to laugh and make others laugh too.
—John Lennon.

• • • •

Elvis with Barbara Stanwyck and
Bud Abbott.
—Photo courtesy of AP Wide
World Photos.

Elvis holding a check for fifty-five
thousand dollars.
—Promotional photograph.

Bud Abbott, and silent film star Chester Conklin participated in the ceremonies.

Elvis didn't limit himself to donating cash. He also gave away items that belonged to him. Anything that he owned was immensely valuable. In 1968 he donated his 1964 Rolls Royce to a women's group for an auction. The organization, SHARE, was founded to aid mentally retarded children.

That same year, he donated his six-door gold Cadillac to an Australian charity appeal. $149,175 was raised for seventeen charities. The Benevolent Society of New South Wales named him an honorary life governor. Elvis had a lot of fans in Australia.

One fan tried to give Elvis a present representing his country — a kangaroo. Elvis loved animals and kept an assortment at Graceland. But a kangaroo was too much to care for. He donated it to the Memphis Zoo.

For many years, Elvis donated the more than ten thousand birthday and Christmas cards he received from his fans to Le Bonheur Children's Hospital. Patients and their parents enjoyed reading them, because, for a time at least, it took their minds off their medical problems.

After filming "Follow That Dream," Elvis and Colonel Parker donated part of the movie set, a shack that had been built on location in Florida to serve as Elvis' rustic beach house. Elvis personally made the donation to the Florida Sheriffs' Boys Ranch, an organization that cared for homeless and neglected youths. It was a group he and Parker had supported several years earlier when they had donated two miniature ponies and a covered wagon. This time Elvis met the boys and talked with them. They were so excited they named the shack after him: the Elvis Presley Canteen. The boys used the small building as a meeting place, and later, when they were grown, renamed it the Elvis Presley Alumni Center. It is still used for reunions.

OPPOSITE:
Elvis with Danny Thomas at the "Potomac" ceremonies.
—Photo courtesy of Graceland.

Elvis seldom had difficulty giving to charity, except when he tried to give away a Presidential yacht. He paid fifty-five thousand dollars at auction for the "Potomac," Franklin D. Roosevelt's floating White House before and during World War II. The 165-foot yacht would have been demolished had Elvis not bought it. Elvis appreciated its historic value and intended to donate the yacht to the March of Dimes Foundation.

Elvis offered the yacht as a national shrine to F.D.R., who had suffered from polio. The March of Dimes raised money to combat this disease, but officials of the organization couldn't justify spending donated funds to maintain the yacht. They declined the offer. Next, Elvis tried to donate the "Potomac" to a Coast Guard auxiliary unit in Miami. The Coast Guard decided the yacht was not appropriate and permission to accept the gift was denied.

A group from North Carolina sent a wire to Elvis requesting the yacht to be used as a war memorial, a companion to the battleship North Carolina which was berthed in Wilmington. Several other organizations asked for the yacht, but Elvis had already made a decision.

The "Potomac" would go to St. Jude Children's Research Hospital. Danny Thomas and Elvis had become friends years before. Impressed with Elvis at his benefit for St. Jude at Russwood Park in 1957, Danny had nicknamed Elvis "Dollface." Later they were to be neighbors in Beverly Hills. Elvis turned to Danny for advice on show business affairs and admired him as a great humanitarian. Their strongest bond was a love for Memphis and for children.

I happen to know, and I know Elvis is too modest to talk about it, but immediately after he purchased the Potomac, he could have sold it at personal profit to himself, but that isn't why he bought it. He bought it with charity in mind.

—Danny Thomas

• • • •

On February 13, 1964, in Long Beach, California, Elvis and Danny met aboard the "Potomac." Elvis formally presented Danny Thomas with the bill of sale. The yacht was again sold and Elvis' donation brought sixty thousand dollars, a sizable contribution to the young hospital.

—Photo courtesy of
St. Jude Children's Research Hospital

Today the "Potomac" is berthed at the Oakland, California, waterfront. A nonprofit organization led by James Roosevelt, the late President's son, is restoring the yacht as a working museum.

Many of Elvis' friends have said that what sets him apart is that he cared. He appreciated all people, not only the rich, the famous, or the beautiful. Elvis once said, "I don't regard money or position as important. It's what a man does that's important."

This was a philosophy Elvis lived by throughout his life, even when his health was poor. While hospitalized at Baptist Hospital for pneumonia, a hospital security guard was wheeling Elvis around the floor. The guard noticed an elderly woman watching for him and told Elvis about her. As Elvis went by her room he waved. Later that day the woman received a note that read, "To Miss Engle, I saw you too. Love, Elvis." He followed up on the note with a bouquet of Hawaiian flowers and visited her several times.

Eighty-four-year-old Miss Engle said she believed Elvis was sent to her from heaven. She was hospitalized for malnutrition but quickly started gaining weight after Elvis' attention. "Imagine him picking out a plain old working girl like me," she said.

But it was working people that Elvis most often helped. Richard Davis remembers an incident that happened in Bel Air. Elvis had eleven friends with him and they had parties every night, sometimes with a hundred girls. Two English girls came to the house often. They were not beautiful but they were nice, and Elvis and his buddies considered them friends. About 3 A.M. the doorbell rang. Everyone was asleep preparing for an early day of film making. Richard opened the door and found these two girls crying hysterically. He brought them inside and tried to calm them down. The girls told him their story.

They had come to Beverly Hills on a work visa. For three years they had saved their money until they had enough to send for

I'm proud of the way that I was brought up to believe and to trust people.

—Elvis

• • • •

—Miss Engle holding a bouquet given to her by Elvis Presley.
—Photo courtesy of the Mississippi Valley Collection, Memphis State University.

their father in England. He had arrived a week ago, and that night had died of a heart attack. All of their savings were gone and they didn't know what they were going to do.

Richard woke Elvis and explained the problem. Elvis quickly responded, "You and Marty (Lacker) take care of it no matter how much it costs. Make sure he has a nice funeral here and then one in England. Be sure and give the girls enough to come back to California."

Several months passed. One morning the doorbell rang and the girls were standing there. They explained they had been working and trying to get back up on their feet. They wanted to see Mr. Elvis. Richard warned them Elvis had just gotten up and didn't see people that early. They insisted they had to see him then. Elvis came to the door and the girls hugged and kissed him. Then they handed him an envelope. When he opened it, tears started streaming down his cheeks. Richard said it was the first time he'd seen Elvis shed tears. As Elvis pulled a five dollar bill from the envelope, the girls said, "We just want to pay you back. This is all we can afford right now." Elvis replied, "No one's ever tried to pay me back. No honey, you keep the money. You've already paid me back more than you'll ever know."

·PART·FOUR·

His Legacy

—Photo courtesy of Linda Everett.

—Photo courtesy of
AP Wide World Photos.

TAKE CARE OF MY FANS

*W*hile many of Elvis' gifts to people were monetary, those that were cherished most were gifts of his time. With a busy career, and countless numbers of people seeking his attention, Elvis never became too famous to attend to his fans. He rarely refused to give an autograph or photograph. He treated each fan as someone very special, often responding to a cry of adoration with, "I love you too, honey." When speaking to an audience, he somehow made them feel as though he was talking personally to each one there.

Elvis was the most successful entertainer of our time; he rarely sang to less than sell-out crowds. It's difficult to pinpoint exactly what it was that Elvis had that separated him from other performers, but what was most different about Elvis was his sincere love of people. His friendliness and concern were a part of his personality, not a pretense for his stage act. Whether performing, visiting with his fans, or corresponding with a sick child, Elvis was always the same. He gave more of himself than any other entertainer has. And his fans responded.

They came from all over the world to Graceland to see him. And the gates were usually open to welcome them. They were allowed to walk up to the first large tree. His friends have said you could always tell when Elvis was outside, because of all the screaming. Elvis would walk down to the gates and allow the waiting crowd to come in. He would sign every autograph patiently, and answer questions. A woman who met Elvis at the gates in 1957 remembers how polite he was. When another girl said to him, "Oh Elvis! You don't know what you do to me!" Elvis responded, "I'm sorry Ma'am, I don't mean to."

Rarely has an entertainer opened his home to his fans. But Elvis was unique. When he was in the mood, he would call the gate and tell the guard to send the crowd of fans up to the house. He would wait until they were all gathered inside, and then sneak into the room to surprise them. "What are you looking at me for?" he'd say.

Elvis felt a rare obligation to his fans. He never took credit for his success, knowing that his fans were responsible for his accomplishments. In many ways, whatever he had was theirs. More than once, an acquaintance of Elvis' would visit him at Graceland and say, "Elvis, are you aware there are people sleeping on your lawn?"

"Yes, Sir. I'm very aware of it," Elvis would answer.

"Did you ever think to call the police?" the bewildered visitor would then ask.

"I'd never do that," Elvis would reply. "These people have come from all over to see me. I wouldn't be in this house if not for them." Trustingly, Elvis wouldn't even lock the doors of his home.

In those days, the lower part of the Graceland lawn was always filled with people. One woman, who discovered Elvis through her teen-age daughter, made many trips from Kansas City to the magical gates. She and a friend would spend two or three days there, sleeping in his yard. It was so much fun, hoping to see Elvis and meeting the other fans who were there for the same reason. Now at seventy-two years of age, she says, "how boring life would have been if we had never had Elvis."

Elvis entertaining a group of young fans in Germany.
—Photo courtesy of Linda Everett.

It wasn't unusual for a fan to spend all of his or her money coming to Memphis. Whenever a guard learned of someone who couldn't afford the trip home, he would call the house and explain the situation to Elvis. The money was always sent to the gate to pay for the bus fare.

The local fans were regulars. One girl followed him so often he came to know her by her nickname, "Inky." One day she spotted him with Natalie Wood, and raced after his car. Elvis, recognizing her, sped through Midtown Memphis, down side streets, and round about, trying to lose her. After all, he was on a date. Inky stayed right behind him, no matter where he turned. Finally, he drove into Overton Park. He started down a dead end road and stopped the car. Inky looked around and saw she was trapped; Elvis was blocking the road ahead and they had driven too far to back up. As Inky sat there, red-faced, Elvis got out of the car and slammed the door. He walked over to her and said very firmly, "Inky, GO HOME." Although she was embarrassed at the time, she laughs about the incident now, and keeps a picture of her and Elvis on display in her home.

Most of the time Elvis enjoyed being followed by his fans. If he was in a particularly playful mood, he might slow his car as he drove onto Elvis Presley Boulevard (U.S. Highway 51 had been renamed in his honor). Almost always, there were fans waiting in their cars to follow him, and they would recognize this signal. He would play a cat and mouse game with them, waiting for them to follow and then speeding up again. Sometimes he would lead them to Whitehaven Plaza Shopping Center, which at this time of night was deserted. He would race around the parking lot doing "donuts," with his fans right behind him.

Elvis never tired of his games with the fans, but slowly, some things at Graceland changed. As the years passed, he required

Every morning when I woke up and looked out the window, there were at least two hundred kids lined up on the sidewalk outside, staring at the house. Some of them would stay there all day long, just trying to get a glimpse of him. And when he would go out, he was very sweet to them. A lot of people I know would get very angry, or impatient—but Elvis is very sweet to the kids, very nice to them. He always spends as much time with them as he can, even though it tires him out.

—Natalie Wood.

• • • •

Many writers have said that his fans worshipped him. Those writers simply used the wrong word. His fans owned him, they were him.

—Jimmy Savile.

• • • •

Elvis stopped at a local gas station and visited with his fans. Here he is with Ann Marie (Buttons) McClain.
—Photo courtesy of
Ann Marie McClain.

more privacy, and stopped allowing the fans past the gates and into his home. He continued to sign autographs, pose for pictures, and race down the boulevard, but less frequently. Nevertheless, there was always a dedicated group of fans at the gates.

Even if Elvis didn't stop his car, his fans might see him as he drove through the gates. When he wasn't in the mood to be photographed, he would raise his left hand to obscure his face. A group of Memphis fans saw this trick many times, and decided to get even. They learned from one of the guards that Elvis would be leaving at a certain time by way of a back exit. The fans stood patiently until Elvis' limousine came into view. Then they turned sideways and raised their left hands to block their faces. Elvis loved it.

He always had a sense of humor with his fans. In concert he would play with them, sporting novelty sunglasses or silly hats.

He would joke with them, telling them he first started moving his hips because his Fruit of the Looms were on too tight. He sometimes changed the lyrics to his songs to make them funny. A favorite game was to sing, "You ain't nothing but a . . ." to which the crowd would applaud enthusiastically. Then he would sing, "You don't know what I'm going to do, you just think you do." Catching the audience completely by surprise, he would break into "You ain't nothin' but an aardvark."

His fans, knowing the opening notes of all of his songs, reacted to the slightest hint of the next number. As the audience would cheer an opening, Elvis would say, "I ain't done nothin' yet. Wait a minute. Honey, what are you screaming for? I've just said, 'Well...' That's all I've done. If that's all I've got to do I've got it made."

For that brief time on stage, he belonged to his fans. They were allowed to go up to the stage, perhaps talk with him for a moment, or give him a gift. And Elvis allowed them to preserve all of their memories on film. His fans were allowed to photograph him as much as they liked. Some fan clubs even hired professional photographers to attend the concerts. Movie cameras, which Colonel Parker didn't approve of, were excluded. And the fans weren't allowed to record the concerts.

While fans could enter the auditoriums with still cameras, they had to conceal their movie cameras and tape recorders. The fines were steep if they were caught filming or recording, but many took the risk. Elvis tried to protect them. He personally didn't object, but he knew what would happen if a security guard discovered the movie cameras or recorders. One fan tells the story of a concert in Las Vegas. She had been sitting in the front row, recording the show, when Elvis walked toward her. She set her recorder down and stared at him. He looked down at her and started motioning for her to look down. She thought, now that I've got him right

In Kansas City one night, I started to sing and six thousand of them ran for the stage. I ran through a door, but they took the door right off the hinges as they came after me. I ran back into the alley where the car was waiting. There was this one right on my heels and when I slammed the door of the car she kept right on coming. Ran her nose right into the door.

—Elvis.

• • • •

Do you think a lot about your fans? I sure do. I always try to conduct my life to set a good example for them. I think about this all the time.

—Elvis
in a 1958 interview.

• • • •

—On-stage in Norfolk, showing off a gift from the Return to Sender Fan Club of Virginia.,

—Photo courtesy of Karen Wilson.

in front of me I'm not going to look away. Elvis started motioning frantically. Finally, she realized he was pointing at her recorder which had become uncovered, and trying to make her understand: the guards are watching. Hide the recorder.

His fans' safety was always Elvis' primary concern. D.J. Fontana recalled, "Elvis was always afraid someone might get hurt at one of his shows. He was afraid the big kids might stomp on the little kids trying to get to the stage. He'd leave the stage if it started to get out of hand." At a show at the Houston Astrodome, Elvis rode around the field in a Jeep, waving at the crowd. Girls scrambled onto the railings trying to get a better look. Elvis said to them, "I'll be up in the balcony a little later on. Don't fall, good God!"

It became a standard line at his concerts. Elvis would say, "I'll make the rounds, just give me a little time," or "Now don't go completely crazy, I'll get around to you," or "Honey, I'll be up there later. See, I've got this grapevine and I'll just swing up there."

Elvis wanted his fans to enjoy themselves. George Klein tells the story of an early stadium concert in Vancouver, Canada. The fans were told to stay in their seats, but they jumped down onto the field as soon as Elvis took the stage. They rushed toward him, and Colonel Parker feared the security might not be able to control the crowd. He pulled Elvis backstage. In a rare moment, Parker took the microphone and told the fans Elvis would come back out if they took their seats again. Backstage, he told Elvis that it looked like a dangerous crowd. "Don't do anything to provoke them," he said.

When Elvis took the stage again, the first thing he did was roll his hips. Then he said to his fans, "Come On Down!" Colonel Parker waited nervously in the wings, but the show went without incident. Still, the Colonel wasn't entirely wrong. Elvis left the stage in his usual manner, sneaking quietly away while his fans waited for an encore. When the crowd realized Elvis wasn't coming back, they rushed for the stage, grabbing sheet music, chairs, and pieces of the stage. Within moments everything was demolished.

His fans wanted any memento of an encounter with Elvis. Once, when he was asked for a souvenir, Elvis said, "I don't have anything. The fans have taken it all." He then looked down at his shoes and

I remember from "Spinout," we were filming a race sequence. A coachload of elderly ladies had pulled up near the stadium. This group just took off across the track toward him—right in front of eleven sports cars racing around the stadium, much of the time at full speed. It was a miracle the drivers didn't hit any of them. Elvis was very concerned about the ladies and went across to them as they were being shepherded back into the bus and very kindly gave each one an autograph.

—Norman Taurog/
Director

• • • •

On-stage at the Houston Astrodome.
—Photo courtesy of Don Wilson.

pulled out a shoelace. In Mobile, Alabama, years later, a man stood up from his front row seat and asked Elvis to autograph a copy of a newspaper. It contained a story of his twenty-hour wait in line to buy tickets for the show. Elvis handed the article to an assistant and started to give the fan a scarf. "I don't want the scarf," the man shouted, "I want that ring!" Inexplicably, Elvis handed him the ring. It was appraised at two thousand dollars.

—Photo courtesy of Don Wilson.

Of course, Elvis is famed for giving away scarves. It was a sure thing, and at every concert the women would gather at the edge of the stage, trying to attract his attention. Even more than the scarf, they wanted the kiss that almost always was given as Elvis draped the scarf around their neck. Elvis knew what his fans wanted but he sometimes asked them: "Honey, what do you want?" A meek voice would answer, "a scarf." He would kiss the girl gently as he placed a scarf around her neck. Then he would say, "Ask and you shall receive." The fans would move in even closer to the stage.

At a show in Monroe, Louisiana, Elvis gave a young girl a scarf, but two older women wrestled it away from her, and started fighting over it. For one of the few times in his life, Elvis was angered on stage. Taking his cross from around his neck, he gave it to the girl. He asked the security guards to escort her out of the building. The necklace was decorated with diamonds and an onyx stone.

It was the young fans that most affected Elvis. Like a great politician, he would pause to kiss a baby or lift a young child onto the stage. Sometimes he would tease the child saying, "Your mama wants a scarf, doesn't she? Did she put you up to this? Here sweetheart, I'll give you one."

There's so much warmth and charm in him that you can't possibly feel from a distance; it's when you're close to him that the real message comes through and you really begin to understand him.
—Myrna Smith/
Singer, Sweet Inspirations

• • • •

As tenderhearted as Elvis was toward children during his performances, his fans rarely witnessed the depth of Elvis' compassion. On tour in Albuquerque, New Mexico, Elvis learned of Denise Sanchez, an eight-year-old girl who was terminally ill with cancer. He met with her during the concert intermission and signed a poster for her. During the performance he dedicated the song, "You Gave Me a Mountain" to her.

Fourteen-year-old Priscilla Myers of Dayton, Ohio, was dying of cystic fibrosis. Priscilla kept calling the radio station and asking them to play Elvis records, and Elvis learned about her through the disc jockey. He gave a concert in Dayton and invited Priscilla and her parents backstage. He kissed Priscilla on the forehead and told her never to give up. Elvis kept in touch with her. Just before she died, almost a year after their meeting, he sent her a telegram and again told her not to ever give up. After her death, he wired his condolences to her parents. Her parents said, "Because of Elvis the last year of her life was the happiest. He had a heart as big as a Cadillac."

On-stage in Norfolk, Virginia.
—Photo courtesy of Karen Wilson.

—Photo courtesy of Karen Wilson.

A young girl from Sweden became the subject of a movie, "To Elvis With Love." Karen was ten years old and dying in an institution for the handicapped. A Hollywood reporter told Elvis about her and said her only dream was to receive a letter from him. Elvis sent her many letters in the months that followed, along with surprise packages of records, photographs, and T-shirts. He always enclosed a note: "To my friend, Karen, from Elvis Presley." In one letter Elvis wrote, "Believe me, I see pretty ladies all the time, and it gets to be a bore. Being real is what counts, and I can tell you are. I am on my way to Nashville to cut a record. If it turns out OK, perhaps I'll send you one. In the meantime, I hope you will write again." Karen died while writing a letter to Elvis. Her last words were, "To Elvis, With Love.

Gary Pepper, a victim of cerebral palsy, was an Elvis fan who hung around the gates of Graceland, in his wheelchair, with his mother or father as an escort. When Elvis returned from Germany, Gary was one of the first people he greeted at the Union Station in Memphis. By that time, Gary had founded the fan club, The Elvis Presley Tankers, in reference to Elvis' duty in the Army.

Elvis took a special interest in Gary, treating him as a friend, not just a fan. Gary was a few years older than Elvis and Elvis looked up to him. In Gary, he sensed enormous inner strength, a refusal to feel sorry for himself, and a dislike for pity. He made others feel special and liked to kid around. To Elvis, Gary was an inspiration. All Gary wanted from Elvis was his friendship, and Elvis reciprocated. He made sure Gary was invited to his New Year's Eve and birthday parties, to his shows in Las Vegas, to Hollywood, and he included him in his all night movie sessions. On one occasion, Elvis took Gary to the Memphis Zoo.

When Gary's father, Sterling Pepper, lost his job, Elvis hired him as a guard. Sometime later, Mr. Pepper died of a heart attack

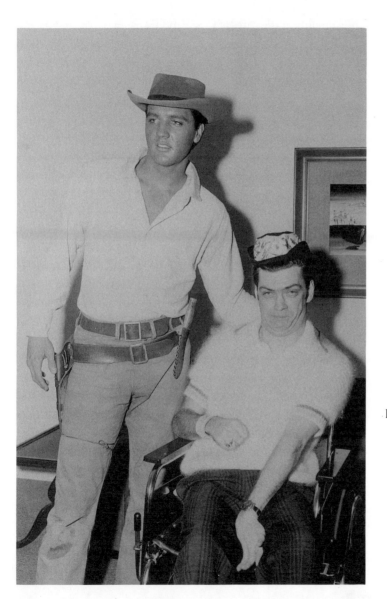

Elvis with his friend Gary Pepper.
—Photo courtesy of Graceland.

while on duty at the gates of Graceland. Elvis, Priscilla, and Vernon went to the Peppers' house to see how they were doing. Elvis asked how their finances were. Then he addressed his father, "Daddy, put Gary on the payroll. We'll make him Fan Club Coordinator and Foreign Correspondent." Elvis hired a full-time assistant to help him and a housekeeper to look after Gary and his mother. Later, he bought their house for them.

Gary pursued his job with a passion, writing letters and magazine articles for fans. Gradually he developed a newspaper clippings service which he operated from his home. He strived to improve himself. When, at the age of forty-five, he learned to drive a car, Elvis purchased a '57 Chevy for him. After Elvis' death, Gary and his mother moved to California where he died in 1980.

Don Wilson is another Elvis fan with a remarkable story. He lost both parents and a sister in a tragic car accident when he was just ten years old. He went to live with his grandmother but his health steadily declined. He was so despondent over the loss of his family, he suffered a nervous breakdown. His depression led to a serious kidney ailment and the doctors offered little encouragement. The only thing that interested him was Elvis' music.

In desperation, his grandmother wrote to Elvis. She told him how worried she was about her grandson and how she felt only Elvis could bring him back to health. Elvis wrote to Don. He sent photos, Christmas cards, records, and Easter cards. Vernon, Priscilla, and members of his staff wrote to encourage him. Don regained his health and his enthusiasm but Elvis never forgot him. The last letter Elvis ever wrote was to his friend, Don. Don has not forgotten. "If I didn't have that going I probably wouldn't have gotten my zest for life back," Don said. "The bottom line is that Elvis cared."

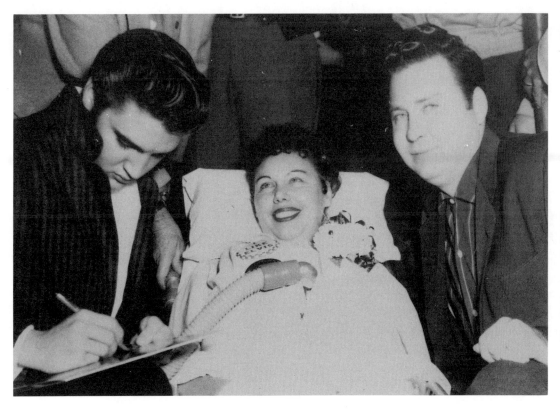

—Photo courtesy of Linda Everett.

THE GREATEST GIFTS
OF ALL

*T*hose who knew Elvis have said he was captivating. He never looked the same twice. His presence was so strongly felt his entrance into a room was known intuitively — before he was seen or heard. A friend of Elvis' recalled a New Year's Eve party and the impact Elvis had on his wife. The woman had never met Elvis and although she hoped to, she wasn't particularly star-struck. In her view, Elvis was just one of the guys her husband hung around with. As the evening wore on she became visibly drunk. Then she was introduced to Elvis. She sobered immediately. Those who were there said it was unbelievable — five cups of coffee couldn't have sobered her. And though she continued to drink throughout the evening, she never became drunk again.

His personal magnetism was commanding, made even more powerful by his desire to make each person feel special with a kind word or a gesture. His charisma transcended the barriers of film and recordings. Elvis cared about people, and his fans, in turn, cared about him. He was a special friend. His fans made him a part of their lives and yearned for personal contact.

When it came to fan reaction, one would think Elvis had seen it all. He watched women hide in dumpsters to catch a glimpse of him. He had seen girls box themselves in crates and ship themselves to Graceland hoping he would open the box. In his twenty-three year career he never understood why his fans loved him so. Even Elvis underestimated his wide appeal.

Richard Davis said, "Elvis knew he was a big star, that he was loved by a lot of people. I don't think he knew how big a star he was or how big a following he had. If he could have seen the people lined up for miles at his funeral, he would have been amazed."

Elvis never recognized his full influence because he thought of himself as just an entertainer. But early in his career he went beyond that role. Several people who knew Elvis have said, "I believe Elvis was put here for a special purpose." His impact was felt in as many ways as there are individuals. For some people his influence was as simple as helping them get through an ordinary work day. For others his power will be felt for a lifetime. He reached deep-rooted needs and desires. Elvis changed lives.

Patsy Andersen, of Graceland, shared a letter written by a woman who was deeply moved by Elvis. The woman was unhappy with her life and thought of killing herself. Little in life brought her satisfaction. She went to the shopping mall, full of despair, contemplating how she would commit the final act. Suddenly, she heard Elvis' voice coming from the record store; they were playing one of his gospel albums. The voice and the words of the song reached out to her. She stopped and listened. And then she knew she had to live. It took time to get her life in order, but she succeeded.

The spiritual songs Elvis recorded are full of emotion and feeling, a testimony to his faith in God. Elvis never evangelized but the sheer power of his recordings, for many people, instilled a desire for a relationship with God.

Elvis' music has reached some tormented souls but the outcome hasn't always been happy. One young woman killed herself while listening to Elvis' music. Her eight-year-old daughter was in the room. The child grew up without her mother and was horribly

Elvis Presley's talent brightened millions of lives. He widened the horizons of my world certainly. The first record I ever owned was a 78 rpm of "Hound Dog" backed by "Don't Be Cruel" and when I listened to those tunes I felt about ten feet tall and I grinned so hard that I felt like the corners of my mouth would meet in the back and the tip of my head would simply topple off. All I know about Rock and Roll is that it makes people feel good. Elvis Presley more than made me feel good, he enriched my life and made it better.

—Stephen King/author.

• • • •

abused. As a teen-ager she became involved with drugs. It seemed her life might end as tragically as her mother's.

Then one day, she heard one of Elvis' songs again. The only real memory she had of her mother were the times she listened to Elvis' music. As the daughter listened to Elvis' singing, she thought about her mother. She also thought of her life and the path she was on. She made the decision to change. Counseling and a lot of hard work put her life in perspective. She overcame her drug abuse and found healthier ways to deal with life.

Elvis provided escape from reality for members of troubled families. In the 1950's and early 1960's divorce wasn't as viable an option for women as it is today. Wives who were beaten or verbally abused by their husbands listened to Elvis' music or watched his movies. He brought them laughter, joy, and hope that things might be better. Sometimes he gave them courage. For those who struggled with divorce, Elvis provided strength. His music was soothing, his image was one of kindness. If a man like Elvis walked this earth, there had to be other men who were caring. It was worth trying for a better life.

Children of troubled homes found comfort in Elvis. When their parents were fighting or were drunk, they could shut themselves in their rooms and listen to Elvis' music. It was almost like being transported to a happier place where there was less pain.

For some, Elvis was a source of comfort when a loved one died. One woman who shared her story with us told of losing her father when she was eleven years old. Her father had been her best friend and without him her life was lonely and empty. Her mother was overcome with grief, unable to attend to her daughter's emotional needs. Her brother was much older and had his own friends and activities. And then she saw Elvis on television. Here was something to get excited about. There were records and magazines to buy. And then his movies to see. He filled the void in her life and brought happiness again.

Pick a word. Influence. Charisma. Meaning. Hope. Example. With any one of those as a subject you could write a whole book on Elvis. So why did he affect so many people? Because Elvis was people.
—Jimmy Savile

• • • •

Even now, after his death, children are discovering Elvis. Most young fans are healthy and happy, but for those who are sick, Elvis helps ease the pain. They can lie in bed and watch his films or listen to his music. He brings them an interest in getting well. They dream of visiting Elvis' home.

For many adult fans Elvis provides strength to endure cancer therapy or other difficult medical procedures. While their families are important to them, the goal to come to Graceland or to attend an Elvis function provides further motivation to get well. Their friends in the Elvis fan network offer support and prayers.

Listening to Elvis' music has, for some fans, aided the healing process. The professional magazine for nurses, *RN*, once featured an article on the benefits of music in treating patients. The story was told of a young woman who had been unresponsive and disoriented. Her parents brought the girl's favorite tapes to the hospital. After listening to Elvis she became calmer and more responsive.

Another Elvis fan was seriously injured by a drunk driver. For six months she lay in a deep coma. Her family tried everything they could think of to get her to respond. Finally, they played Elvis' music. Success! She wiggled her toe. They had found something she was interested in. Next, they required her to move her foot before they would let her hear Elvis' music. Today, the coma is far behind her. Full recovery is slow but she is alert and enjoying Elvis.

Elvis was an inspiration to many; one doctor admits he achieved his goals to become a physician because of Elvis. He too was from a poor community, and his childhood was much like Elvis'. Elvis was a role model to him. The fact that Elvis could reach his goals, given the same background, provided him with the inspiration to fight for his dreams. He put himself through medical school and succeeded.

I enjoy myself when I'm singing. I put my whole heart into it, you know? I believe in my music strongly enough, so that it shows. The kids know that. I enjoy my singing and they like that. The way I look at it, if my music helps the kids enjoy life, why, I'm mighty glad.

—Elvis.

•　•　•　•

Elvis has inspired people in all countries. For some, Elvis was the motivation to learn the English language. They wanted to understand the words he was singing. His effect on world culture is staggering. At a meeting of the Council of Europe, one spokesman said that Elvis, by providing a common focus for European youth, had done more to unite Europe than the council members. Musically, Elvis united the world. Country or status has little bearing. The working man in England, the President of Zimbabwe, the teen-ager in Texas, and the Queen of Thailand all share a common interest . . . Elvis Presley.

We could continue to tell of the way Elvis touched his fans. No one can tell their stories better than they can. Here are a few of the memories shared with us:

From a fan in England:

> . . . *I always felt that Elvis was someone special; he wasn't just a singer or pop idol but for many years I didn't know quite what it was. Then some years ago my marriage broke up. It was after Elvis' death and I prayed for his help and guidance. It worked and it helped me no end.*

• • • •

From Greece:

> *Elvis is no doubt the King of the Sound of Music . . . of yesterday, today, tomorrow, and FOREVER. A marvelous young man . . . . A man who really cared . . . . He shared . . . . Not only did he touch the lives of Greeks but of all human races from North to South, East to West . . . God, how we miss him.*

• • • •

From an American fan

. . . Elvis did make a difference in my life. That difference goes back to 1956 when my brother and I saw "Love Me Tender." He still makes a difference in my life. It is through Elvis that I have met so many new friends. Everyone that I have corresponded with is so friendly and close. The feeling to share is real . . . . What matters about Elvis is: Does he add joy to our lives? Does he make you feel good, not only about yourself but others? Did he give us something precious? Yes, yes . . . .

• • • •

From a fan battling leukemia:

. . . I have been planning my fifth fan club convention for charity. I know with God's help I'll make it through. Can't let the children down or the fans. Have to keep Elvis' name flowing as the caring and loving man he was.

• • • •

From a fan in Texas

. . . At the age of eleven I became a "die-hard" Elvis fan. Watching "Elvis - That's the Way It Is" just blew my mind. Never had I seen an entertainer like him who would pour out his heart and soul in his songs for his fans and express that much love and gratitude. All that took place in 1977, on August 17 — one day after he had passed away. But in my heart I knew he would never die. His soul had touched me too deeply. My father died in 1976 — Elvis became my surrogate dad, friend, and brother whenever I wished him to be with me. Over the years I thought it would go away, my feelings for Elvis, since I was still a kid when I got fascinated with him. Usually everything faded away after that period of my life. But not Elvis! It became more and

---

He made people feel like someone loved them.

—Marty Lacker.

• • • •

more intense, it was like growing up with Elvis. I needed his voice, songs and gorgeous pictures to look at more than ever before. Especially his spirituals soothe me in times of personal trouble. Whenever I'm blue I watch one of my favorite shows on video and always feel much better.

• • • •

From another loyal fan

. . . For years I have wanted to go to Graceland but for the past twenty years I have suffered with anxiety attacks. Each year I would cancel out. I just could not face the fact of leaving the safety of being close to my home. One year I made up my mind I desperately had to see the places where Elvis lived and where he found such peace. His music and videos have been like a prescription drug for me for years now so I had to go visit his grave and tell him of my love for him and thank him for pulling me through some bad times.

Along came February and the deposit was due. Then came June and I paid off the trip, but when August came I started to get scared, but I took one day at a time, and found that on August 9, my dream was happening. I was on my way to Graceland! From the moment I reached its walls, I could feel the love and peace all around me. My first night I went to the Meditation Gardens and cried and said my thanks to Elvis. I was truly at peace with myself for the first time in a long time. I can truly say it was one of the highlights of my life.

So if you want something bad enough, you get the courage to face any obstacle.

• • • •

From Malta

. . . I've been an Elvis fan since my youth back in the late '50's. When I feel down I always play Elvis' music or put an Elvis film in the VCR and I can always relax and feel much better.

• • • •

The greatest gift any person can give to another is a part of himself and Elvis gave this as few others have.

—Jim Hannaford.

• • • •

From a fan in Pennsylvania

. . . Being an Elvis fan has certainly enriched my life. In 1987 I found myself in a body cast with six broken vertebrae. Some nights I found it impossible to sleep, so I would get up and put a video or a cassette on and I would get totally lost in his actions, he could almost draw me into him. I could feel his songs and what they were all about, anyway it was enough to lose myself and forget my pain.

Since then I find myself turning to him daily. The following year I suffered a broken rib and in November of '90 had an emergency surgery done, discovered I had another serious condition, but I find turning to Elvis takes my mind off things. I have met so many people who share my feelings and we keep in touch, he has opened so many doors to me. Elvis was given a God-given talent and he certainly didn't let Him down; he used it to help so many people all in different ways and yet in the same way somehow. He united a whole world of people.

• • • •

From a fan in Florida

. . . I was only fifteen when I was asked to leave home. All I took with me were my clothes, record player, and my Elvis records. I lived in half a room. More than before I turned to

Elvis for comfort. He has always been my strength and I have never had an unhappy day as he has a song for each of us. He was a God-given gift to us. It always brings a smile to my face when I am at Graceland and there are people from around the world who can not speak any English but they can say "Elvis" loud and clear. Elvis continues to bridge the gap between countries. I get upset and miss Elvis above all else but then I think about what would be really sad is if there had never been an Elvis . . .

• • • •

· C H A P T E R · XIII ·

THE LEGACY
CONTINUES

AUGUST 16, 1977. Even those who weren't Elvis' strongest fans were stunned by the news: Elvis was dead. Radio announcers played tributes to Elvis, and television broadcasters introduced their news programs with the late-breaking story. Politicians, musicians, and celebrities released statements about the loss of Elvis and of his influence on them. It was the end of an era, and a reminder of everyone's mortality. His fans grieved.

By the next day, so many mourners had purchased floral arrangements, Memphis florists had run out of flowers. It was the single largest day in FTD history. Elvis Presley Boulevard was the focus of national attention. Thousands traveled from across the country to say good-bye. Unable to find a hotel room, they maintained their vigil in front of Graceland, sleeping on the sidewalk. Many stood in line for hours for a chance to view his body. For weeks after his burial, his fans continued to come to Memphis.

In 1978, one year after his death, many fans returned to honor Elvis. It was the impromptu beginning of a tradition, "Elvis Presley International Tribute Week" (in 1992 renamed "Elvis Week"), held every August. In 1982, Graceland, the estate of Elvis Presley, opened the home for tours and became active in Tribute Week, sponsoring and sanctioning fund-raisers to assist specific charities.

Each year an auction of Elvis memorabilia raises money for Le Bonheur Children's Hospital. The hospital also receives the proceeds from the Elvis Presley Memorial Karate Tournament which is in its ninth year. The Elvis Presley Memorial Trauma Center has sponsored softball games and plans a riverboat auction on the Mississippi River. The Elvis Presley International 5K Run is an annual event begun in 1983 to benefit United Cerebral Palsy. 1989 was the first year of the annual Elvis Presley Memorial Dinner To Benefit the Make A Wish Foundation.

Graceland, along with The Then, Now And Forever Fan Club of Memphis, have adopted Humes Junior High School, Elvis' alma mater. They are members of the Memphis Adopt A School Program and they channel their fund-raising efforts to benefit the school. Graceland purchased a stage curtain for the auditorium, renamed in honor of Elvis. The club operates a gift shop in one of the classrooms to raise money for the school and it helped restore two classrooms in the 1950's style. During the week, tours of the classrooms and auditorium are given. Many of Elvis' family and friends gather for a symposium at Humes and share remembrances with the fans. Graceland plans to endow a college scholarship for a Humes graduate to study music.

During the year Graceland continues to support charity. They support the Shelby United Way, St. Jude Childrens' Research Hospital, the Elvis Presley Memorial Trauma Center and many other organizations. In December Elvis Presley's estate encourages fans to participate in Elvis' tradition of decorating his home for the holidays. Each year since 1982, fans have purchased poinsettias which adorn Graceland. Proceeds from the flower sales benefit the Memphis Chapter of the National Hemophilia Foundation.

The banquet held in honor of Elvis' birthday (January 8) each year benefits a variety of causes. In January 1991, the theme of

—Photo courtesy of Linda Everett.

the program was Elvis' performance to benefit the USS Arizona. The gold lamé suit Elvis had worn at that concert was on display. The United States flag, given to Elvis by the Navy, was draped in the background. The United States Navy Band, dressed in full uniform, honored Elvis with a moving arrangement of patriotic music. Graceland donated the admission tickets from the 1991 banquet to the care of the USS Arizona Memorial.

The staff of Graceland does more than give money. One of their favorite charities is the Johns Hopkins Children's Cancer Foundation in Baltimore, Maryland. In 1987, they were asked to participate in a fund-raising event for the hospital. Patsy Andersen recalls that she and Jerry Schilling represented Graceland. They met some of the children and were particularly moved by two very sick seven-year-olds who loved Elvis. Patsy and Jerry decided to bring them to Graceland for the grand tour. One of the children spent three days there and even visited the stable and Elvis' horses. Then Graceland packed the child's bags full of souvenirs to remember the trip. He died later that year. Patsy is grateful for her role in making his wish come true. She and many of Elvis' friends support this charity and similar causes.

His friends, like Elvis, are reluctant to talk about their good deeds. They "do what they can to help," Richard Davis says. "If you were around him it rubbed off on you. He was so loving and caring. As his valet, I used to buy a lot of his clothes for him. He gave me a lot of them. I've given all of it away to charities."

George Klein does more for charity than any other of Elvis' friends because, as a radio and television celebrity, he's often asked to participate in telethons and other fund-raisers. George never refuses. He's been honored by the Epilepsy Foundation, United Cerebral Palsy, and many other organizations he has supported. Each December George sponsors a charity show and auction to

To me and to the charities which have benefitted from this spirit of goodwill and brotherhood, this is the most wonderful thing about Elvis. I have never failed to wonder at the atmosphere of goodwill wherever his admirers are gathered.

—Todd Slaughter.

• • • •

Elvis' following was immense, and he was a symbol to the people of the world of the vitality, rebelliousness, and good humor of this country. Elvis may be gone, but his legend will be with us for a long time.

—President Jimmy Carter.

• • • •

benefit the Memphis Inter-Faith Association, which operates the Memphis Food Bank. The show, which is in its twenty-eighth year, features celebrity performers such as Jerry Lee Lewis, Linda Gail Lewis, The Drifters, The Coasters, and many others. For George's first benefit, Anita Wood and Ace Cannon appeared.

Elvis' fans are diligent in their efforts to raise money. There are raffles or souvenir sales to benefit charity at fan gatherings. Most fan clubs sponsor annual functions such as conventions, auctions, dinners, and dances. Other events throughout the year include Elvis memorabilia sales, bingo games, Tupperware sales, and children's parties. Some clubs have published books and donated the proceeds to a favorite charity.

Some Elvis fans have, on occasion, endured ridicule for their passion. Robin Rosaaen, Public Relations Liaison for The Elvis Special Photo Association of California, made an appearance on "The Oprah Winfrey Show" in 1991. On the air, Robin described her collection of Elvis memorabilia which she values at a quarter of a million dollars. Oprah reacted in disbelief and an audience member declared she had wasted her money.

What they didn't know is that Robin uses her collection to raise money for charity. In 1990 she staged a three-day exhibit of her memorabilia at a San Francisco Bay area hotel. Adults were charged five dollars and children two dollars to see her collection. Robin donated proceeds of the exhibit to the Peninsula Volunteers programs for the elderly. Another display in April 1992 benefitted Meals On Wheels.

Bill De Night, president of The Elvis Presley Burning Love Fan Club in Streamwood, Illinois, is dedicated to raising money for charity. Bill is a rare individual. He and his wife, Noreen, work an average of sixty hours a week for Elvis' memory. Even Christmas day is no exception. Bill has an extensive collection of memorabilia

Then, as now, and in years to come, those who try to understand the Presley magic by judging his songs and films will miss the point completely. The point is for twenty years and for many millions of people, Elvis was like a relative. He was our twin brother that was doing well.

—Jimmy Savile.

• • • •

and has donated many items to his club's auctions. Bill says, "Every item I own is very precious to me but not as precious as preserving Elvis' memory. I don't believe in recognition. Elvis never asked for recognition. I do it because it's so rewarding."

His efforts have brought Burning Love the honor of being the largest contributor to charity in Elvis' memory in the world. Each year Bill's goal is to raise the amount of money corresponding with the number of years since Elvis' passing. On the fifteenth anniversary, his goal is to raise fifteen thousand dollars. Donations are made monthly and are split equally between the Elvis Presley Memorial Trauma Center and Le Bonheur Children's Hospital.

Wilma and Robert Wooten, of Welcome, North Carolina, own a printing company. They have published a series of cookbooks, "The Elvis Fans Cookbook," as a fund-raising project to benefit the Elvis Presley Memorial Trauma Center. Wilma has collected recipes from Elvis fans around the world. The cookbooks are sold at Graceland, at fan club gatherings, and at other Elvis-related events. To date the Wootens have published four cookbooks. Wilma has said, "The charity work the fans are doing is one of the most positive ways to keep the memory of Elvis alive."

Because of the efforts of Shelby County Mayor Bill Morris, the Elvis Presley Memorial Trauma Center at the Regional Medical Center at Memphis is the only institution in the world named for Elvis Presley. The Regional Medical Center is the oldest hospital in the city. It was founded in 1829 as John Gaston Hospital and cared for itinerant travelers on the Mississippi River. It has always been a city hospital committed to providing the best health care regardless of the patient's ability to pay. Today the hospital has several Centers of Excellence to care for specific medical problems. There are centers for high-risk obstetrics, newborns, burns, and trauma. In November 1983, the Trauma Center was dedicated. It

All rock and roll is communication and that's something that's never out of style. Still, it's real mind-boggling sometimes to think of how rock and roll enabled us to bring this big world a little closer together.

—Sam Phillips.

•   •   •   •

is equipped to care for life-threatening injuries, making it the only Level 1 facility in the Mid-South.

The Elvis Presley Memorial Trauma Center Advisory Cabinet is a group of Elvis Fan Club presidents and others who are committed to promoting the Trauma Center. Their efforts have brought worldwide attention to the facility. The fans support the Trauma Center's work and their appreciation of Elvis. Over $125,000 has been given to the charity. Donations come in from countries all over the world, in amounts ranging from one dollar to thousands of dollars. Some fans support this organization exclusively. Their work has been rewarded. In August 1990, a wall of honor was unveiled at the Elvis Presley Memorial Trauma Center in recognition of the most generous fans. Each plaque on the wall of honor represents cumulative donations of a thousand dollars or more.

I believe I will see Elvis Presley in heaven.

—Billy Graham.

• • • •

St. Jude Children's Research Hospital is one of the fifty organizations listed on Elvis' plaque in the Graceland trophy room. Danny Thomas opened St. Jude Children's Research Hospital in 1962, naming it after the patron saint of lost causes. The hospital was established to treat cancers and other catastrophic illnesses afflicting children. Danny Thomas operated the hospital on the principles that no child should die before his or her time, that no child should be denied treatment because of inability to pay, and that the research results should be available worldwide.

Each day tremendous strides are made in research, and many children are alive because of Danny Thomas' effort. When the hospital first opened, the success rate for treating acute lymphocytic leukemia was four percent. Today, the cure rate for the disease is seventy-three percent. St. Jude Children's Research Hospital is recognized worldwide.

Elvis had planned to visit the children at St. Jude after his August 1977 tour. Unfortunately, he never made that visit. Im-

—Photo courtesy of Linda Everett.

mediately after Elvis' death hundreds of contributions were made to the hospital in his memory. Fans from around the world continue to support St. Jude. The Love 4 Elvis Fan Club of Clifton, New Jersey, sponsors an annual auction to benefit the hospital. For many years a fan club in Belgium has sent a large contribution in Belgian currency.

On February 6, 1991, Danny Thomas died in his California home. He had returned from fund-raising appearances in Memphis earlier that day. To the end of his life Danny Thomas worked for the children of St. Jude. He was buried in a crypt within the pavilion on the hospital grounds. In the center of the pavilion the walls are covered with memorabilia from Danny's career, his awards, and photographs of him and his friends. Amid all of the pictures of Hollywood celebrities, there's a picture of Danny and his friend, Elvis, aboard the "Potomac."

The Le Bonheur Children's Medical Center was founded by the Le Bonheur Club and the Memphis Pediatric Fund in 1952. The hospital's objective is to "do whatever it takes to make the hurt go away." Le Bonheur provides services to all children who need it, regardless of ability to pay. Elvis visited the hospital occasionally and remembered the charity each Christmas with a donation. In 1966 Mrs. John Thompson, President of the Le Bonheur Club, said of him, "I think this is one of the great things about Elvis. He always remembers his home and the charities in need." His fans continue to support Le Bonheur.

One Christmas after Elvis' death, James and Betty Page brought dolls and stuffed animals to the children at Le Bonheur. During the year the Pages collected items from other fans to donate to the hospital. Eventually their efforts developed into an annual auction. Today Elvis' fans have donated more than one hundred thousand dollars to Le Bonheur.

Porter Leath Children's Home is an organization that Elvis remembered nearly every Christmas. Today, fans from around the world support Porter Leath. Teddy bears are collected for the children. Fan club newsletters ask fans to "do it for the children and do it in loving memory of Elvis Aaron Presley." Each year on January 8, Elvis' birthday, a party is given for the children and the stuffed animals are distributed.

Graceland encourages fans to support charities in their own communities. While it's nice to see donations pour into Memphis from all over the world, charitable needs are found everywhere.

Alice Schlichte, of Renton, Washington, sponsors the Elvis Lives On Fan Convention each September. The project was begun to thank Elvis for the happiness he's given all of his fans. The convention benefits children's needs and donations have been made to Special Olympics, the University of Washington Research Center in the Department of Pediatrics, New Horizon Ministries which provides care to homeless children, and other charities. Despite poor health, Alice is dedicated to assisting children in Elvis' name. She said, "Elvis was so warm and caring. The public should never forget this. In Elvis' name I give, and with the help of the Elvis fans we make this all come true."

The We Remember Elvis Fan Club of Pittsburgh, Pennsylvania, is committed to "ensuring Elvis is not forgotten through charity work in his memory." This club supports a variety of organizations. The March of Dimes, the Children's Hospital of Pittsburgh, various local food banks, and the Elvis Presley Memorial Trauma Center have received contributions. The fan club has also created a lasting gift named after Elvis.

The Elvis Aaron Presley Visiting Fellowship at the West Penn Hospital's Burn and Trauma Unit was founded in 1989 to educate medical personnel in the treatment of burn injuries. The first

The amount of a fan club's charitable contributions is not as important as the spirit of giving.
—Patsy Andersen.

• • • •

recipient of the fellowship was Dr. Amiram Borenstein from Israel, who learned newly-developed techniques to take back to his own country. In 1991 the club brought a doctor and two nurses from England to study. The exchange of information provided by this fellowship is an ongoing memorial to Elvis.

The We Remember Elvis Fan Club has been commended by the mayor of Pittsburgh and the Governor of Pennsylvania for their efforts. On April 21, 1990, the city of Pittsburgh proclaimed Elvis Presley Day to focus attention on the fan club's fund-raising effort, their ninth annual fan convention.

The Elvis Country Fan Club of Austin, Texas, sponsors the Elvis Presley Performing Arts Scholarship each year. Since 1985, scholarships of a thousand dollars are given annually to graduating high school seniors who plan a career in the performing arts. Through the gift of education, talented individuals are aided in reaching their goals.

For more than fourteen years Peggy Sue Sosebee of Atlanta has sponsored a Teddy Bear Caravan for the children of the Scottish Rite Hospital. She collects stuffed bears from fans throughout the United States and Canada to deliver each Christmas. Several hundred bears are brought to the hospital, loaded on stretchers, and distributed to children in all departments of the hospital.

There are many more fans working for charity than can be listed here. Monetary success is not always a measure of effort or will, because it may be due to an individual or an organized endeavor. Some fan clubs raise more money than others but have the advantage of a large membership to share the work. Others live in metropolitan areas where attendance at events is greater. A small club in a rural area might expend as much time and energy raising a small amount of money as a larger club spends in raising thousands of dollars. Regardless of the results, the spirit of giving is the same.

You don't have to say Elvis Presley. You say Elvis, and everyone knows him. Look at the response that we get from people all over the world and it continues to grow so many years after.

—Pat Patterson.

• • • •

I hope people remember the impact. It's not only historical fact, but it's definitely lingering fact.
—Roy Orbison.

• • • •

In nearly every corner of the world, something nice is being done for someone else in Elvis' name. Charity is more than supporting a specific cause; it also includes acts of kindness. Elvis' fans support each other. They are an extended family, full of love and warmth. When a member of the TCB Fan Club in Georgia struggled to survive cancer, the club raised over twenty-four hundred dollars to assist with her medical bills. Elvis fans from around the world remembered her in their prayers and thoughts.

There are many stories of fans who have suffered fires and have lost their belongings. Other Elvis fans have donated money, clothing, household items, and even Elvis memorabilia to help make up for the loss. But it isn't only other Elvis fans that they respond to. They try to help anyone in need. If they hear of a tragedy that's befallen someone, they donate money or time either individually or in an organized effort.

Today there are over two hundred eighty Elvis Presley fan clubs throughout the world. The number continues to grow as more people are introduced to Elvis. Young people who do not remember him while he was alive have become fans after seeing his movies or concerts on television. Elvis captures new audiences in formerly Communist countries. Fan clubs exist now in Russia, Czechoslovakia, and other countries where only a few years ago freedom to choose did not exist. Even in the People's Republic of China, which remains a dictatorship, the '68 Comeback Special was chosen by fans given the opportunity to choose any television program.

Fan club traditions vary among different cultures. American fans seem to feel a great responsibility toward Elvis and toward charity. They view Elvis as an inspiration and want other people to remember him as they do, as a humanitarian. They strive to see that Elvis is not forgotten.

Efforts for national recognition have been underway for many years. Kathy and John Ferguson have led a campaign to honor

Elvis with a national "Elvis Presley Day." At long last, Congressman Glen Anderson of Long Beach, California, has offered to introduce this bill.

Pat Geiger is celebrating a hard-earned victory. For nine years she struggled to persuade the United States Postal Service to issue a stamp with Elvis' likeness. Thousands of fans supported her efforts and the Postmaster General received 50,000 signatures and tens of thousands of letters. The stamp will be issued on January 8, 1993.

Some European clubs have been less service-oriented than American fan clubs. They hold dances, parties, and other social functions. Although fewer foreign clubs have adopted charitable causes than American fan clubs, this seems to be changing. More and more international fans are becoming involved in fund-raising efforts. The philosophy of carrying on Elvis' work is becoming a worldwide tradition.

It's impossible to speculate on the amount of money raised in Elvis' name, how many people have been helped, or the number of charities supported. Like Elvis, many of his fans aren't concerned with publicity. Their work is not for recognition, it's for something greater; a love of people, and, especially, a love for Elvis Presley.

Appendix

For those interested in making charitable donations in Elvis' name,
the following addresses may be helpful.

THE ELVIS PRESLEY MEMORIAL TRAUMA CENTER
THE MED Foundation
877 Jefferson Avenue
Memphis, TN 38103

LE BONHEUR CHILDREN'S HOSPITAL
One Children's Plaza
Memphis, TN 38103

PORTER LEATH CHILDREN'S CENTER
868 N. Manassas
Memphis, TN 38107

ST. JUDE CHILDREN'S RESEARCH HOSPITAL
ALSAC
501 St. Jude Place
Memphis, TN 38105

Bibliography

Burk, Bill, E. Early *Elvis: The Humes Years*. Memphis: Burk Enterprises, 1990.

— —*Elvis Through My Eyes*. Memphis: Burk Enterprises, 1987.

Cotten, Lee. *All Shook Up*. Ann Arbor: Pierian Press, 1985.

Doll, Susan, ed. *Elvis: A Tribute To His Life*. Newark: Beekman House, 1989.

Farren, Mick, and Pearce Marchbank, comps. *Elvis In His Own Words*. London: Omnibus Press, 1977.

Gregory, Neal, and Janice Gregory. *When Elvis Died*. Washington: Communications Press, 1980.

Haining, Peter, ed. *Elvis In Private*. New York: St. Martin's Press. 1987.

Hannaford, Jim. *Elvis Golden Ride On The Mystery Train*. self-published, 1986.

Hodge, Charlie, with Charles Goodman. *Me'n Elvis*. Memphis: Castle Books, 1988.

Hopkins, Jerry. *Elvis: A Biography*. New York: Warner Books, 1972.

Jenkins, Mary, with Beth Pease. *Elvis Memories Beyond Graceland Gates*. Buena Park, CA: West Coast Publishing, 1989.

Loper, Karen. *Elvis Clippings*. self-published, n.d.

Loyd, Harold. *Elvis Presley's Graceland Gates*. Franklin, TN: Jimmy Velvet Publications, 1987.

Nash, Alanna. *Behind Closed Doors*. New York: Knopf, 1988. (Minnie Pearl interview, pp. 397-419)

Parker, Ed. *Inside Elvis*. Orange, CA: Rampart House, 1979.

Presley, Priscilla, with Susan Harmony. *Elvis and Me*. New York: Berkeley Books, 1986.

Presley, Vester, with Deda Bonura. *A Presley Speaks*. Memphis: Wimmer Bros., 1978.

Rijff, Ger. *Long Lonely Highway: A 1950's Elvis Scrapbook*. Ann Arbor: Pierian Press, 1987.

Shaw, Sid. *Elvis In Quotes*. London: Elvisly Yours, Inc., n.d.

Taylor, Roger, ed. *Elvis In Art*. New York; St. Martin's Press. 1987.

Westmoreland, Kathy. *Elvis and Kathy*. Glendale, CA: Glendale House Publishing, 1987.

Worth, Fred L., and Steve D. Tamerius. *Elvis: His Life From A To Z*. Chicago: Contemporary Books, 1990.

Magazines

Burk, Bill, E., and Connie Burk, eds. *Elvis World*. Memphis: Burk Enterprises. 1989-1991.

Graceland Express. 1990-1991. Memphis: An official publication of Graceland - a Division of Elvis Presley Enterprises, Inc.

Lamm, Darwin, ed. *Elvis International Forum*. 1989-1991. Thousand Oaks, CA: Creative Radio Network.

Parker, Priscilla, ed. *We Remember Elvis Fan Club Newsletter*. 1989-1992. Pittsburgh: We Remember Elvis Fan Club.

Polwert, Steve, ed. *Elvis*. Vol 1-4. 1990. St. Louis: After Midnight Press.

Smith, Billy, ed. *Elvis The Record*. Memphis: Smith-Lacker-Davis, Inc. 1980.

Video

Abel, Robert, and Pierre Adige, directors. *Elvis On Tour*. MGM. Cinema Associates Production. 1972.

Elvis: Aloha From Hawaii Via Satellite. RCA; NBC. First broadcast on U. S. television, January 14, 1973.

Morgan, Todd. Letter to authors, February 20, 1991, containing "More Than Cadillacs and Diamond Rings," unpublished video script by the staff of Graceland, Memphis.

Raymond, Alan, and Susan Raymond, directors. *Elvis '56*. Los Angeles: Media Home Entertainment Co., 1987.

Sanders, Dennis, director. *Elvis: That's The Way It Is*. MGM, 1970.

Solt, Andrew, executive producer. *Elvis: The Great Performances*, Vol. 1: *Center Stage*. Vol 2: *The Man and The Music*. Burbank, CA: Buena Vista Home Video, 1991.

Perhaps it's not an accident that Mike Freeman and Cindy Hazen began writing a book about Elvis. As residents of Memphis, they had, individually, watched the Elvis phenomenon from an affectionate distance. Too young to experience Elvis' impact in the fifties, they took Elvis for granted — as most Memphians do.

But something happened when Mike and Cindy met. Not only did they fall in love; they found common interests in music, writing and research. And they were curious about Elvis. What was it that brought so many people to Memphis?

While trying to answer that question, they fell into the trap many writers fear; they lost their objectivity. Because they found out what Elvis' fans had known all along — he was a powerful entertainer and a remarkable man.

The Best of Elvis is their second project. In 1990 they released "The Whole Elvis Tour, A Pocket Guide to the King's Memphis." They are now working on a full-sized volume on Elvis Presley's Memphis, and a volume on Tupelo. Their adventures are just beginning. Mike and Cindy are continuing to collect stories of Elvis' generosity and his impact on his fans. If you have a story you would like to share, or if you want to comment on "The Best of Elvis", write to Mike and Cindy:

c/o Memphis Explorations
P.O. Box 41134
Memphis, TN 38174